Crock Pot Cookbook for Beginners

1000 Easy and Mouthwatering Recipes for Everyday Crock Pot Cooking Paperback

Cathryn Brent

CONTENTS

Appetizers Recipes 26

Beef, Pork & Lamb Recipes 29

Fish & Seafood Recipes

Lunch & Dinner Recipes 61

Side Dish Recipes 81

Snack Recipe 85

Dessert Recipes 91

Introduction

What is a Crock-Pot?

A slow cooker, also known as a crock-pot, is a countertop electrical cooking device used for simmering at a lower temperature than other cooking methods such as baking, boiling and frying. This facilitates unattended cooking of many hours of dishes that would otherwise require boiling: pot roasts, soups, stews and other dishes, including beverages, desserts and dips.

Tips for using a crock pot

Crock pots can prepare any type of dish you can imagine, including accompanying side dishes, breads and desserts. You don't have to worry about the food; it doesn't require constant attention or stirring. (In fact, unless the recipe says otherwise, you should not remove the lid while cooking, as the leaking heat will add almost another 30 minutes to the cooking time.)

Slow cookers are, of course, ideal for the soups and stews mentioned above, and they're especially good for dishes that require tougher, cheaper meats. But consider using your slow cooker for side dishes and desserts, too. This is especially helpful if you're entertaining and your oven may be occupied by another long-cooking dish; in this case, use your slow cooker as another oven or burner.

To make cleanup easier, spray the inside of the pot with a non-stick cooking spray before adding food.

Meat will not brown in the slow cooker, so recipes for meats that need to brown will instruct you to brown the meat in the pan before adding it to the slow cooker.

Slow cooking does not lose moisture as traditional cooking methods do, so - as much as you may be tempted to do so - do not add more liquid to the pan than the recipe calls for.

Remember that the cooking times in all recipes are approximations. Several factors can affect cooking time - the qualities of your slow cooker, how much food is in the pot, the humidity, the temperature at which you add the ingredients - so be aware that the cooking time in a recipe is only a range.

Don't leave a finished dish in the slow cooker for very long. It will continue to cook for a while, which may overcook the food; then, as the slow cooker cools, the food will not stay warm enough to prevent bacterial growth. Again, don't use the slow cooker to reheat; the slow cooker only gradually reaches cooking temperature, which gives bacteria a chance to grow.

Crock pot Cooker Knowledge

The Crock pot cooker is a versatile device for both vegetarian and meat and poultry, everyday meals and entertaining occasions. You can create hearty, healthy dishes for the whole family in a "ready-to-use" format. Simply add ingredients to your slow cooker, continue your day and come home to a kitchen filled with inviting aromas.

A Crock pot cooker, essentially an electric pot with a stoneware liner, can do what an oven or stove top can't: cook food at a consistently low and even temperature, possibly for up to 10 or 12 hours. When you're out and about, dinner is already cooked.

The taste is one of the biggest advantages of cooking in your pan. You can end up with a flavorful dish at the end of an 8- or 10-hour slow cooker. Saving time is another reason for the popularity of slow cookers. Plus, they're practical: Since slow cookers can hold up to five quarts, you can definitely plan to eat leftovers.

However, this also involves planning. Slow cookers are great for inexpensive cuts of meat that require long, gentle cooking to tenderize: beef ribs, brisket, pork shoulder and leg of lamb. However, the same cannot be said for fish and dairy products; both break down during the cooking process. Chicken can also soften, so pay strict attention to the cooking time of chicken recipes.

Always put the vegetables in first. Vegetables take longer to cook than meat, so for layering purposes, put the vegetables in first, then the meat, and finally the dressing and a small amount of liquid. To prevent overcooking, add fresh dairy products, pasta or instant rice during the last 30 minutes of cooking time, or as the recipe calls for.

Breakfast Recipes

Bacon Eggs

Servings:2
Cooking Time: 2 Hours
Ingredients:
- 2 bacon slices
- 2 eggs, hard-boiled, peeled
- ¼ teaspoon ground black pepper
- 1 teaspoon olive oil
- ½ teaspoon dried thyme

Directions:
1. Sprinkle the bacon with ground black pepper and dried thyme.
2. Then wrap the eggs in the bacon and sprinkle with olive oil.
3. Put the eggs in the Crock Pot and cook on High for 2 hours.

Nutrition Info:
- Per Serving: 187 calories, 12.6g protein, 0.9g carbohydrates, 14.7g fat, 0.2g fiber, 185mg cholesterol, 501mg sodium, 172mg potassium.

Chicken Meatballs

Servings:4
Cooking Time: 4 Hours
Ingredients:
- 3 tablespoons bread crumbs
- 1 teaspoon cream cheese
- 10 oz ground chicken
- 1 tablespoon coconut oil
- 1 teaspoon Italian seasonings

Directions:
1. Mix bread crumbs with cream cheese, ground chicken, and Italian seasonings.
2. Make the meatballs and put them in the Crock Pot.
3. Add coconut oil and close the lid.
4. Cook the chicken meatballs for 4 hours on High.

Nutrition Info:
- Per Serving: 190 calories, 21.2g protein, 3.8g carbohydrates, 9.6g fat, 0.2g fiber, 65mg cholesterol, 101mg sodium, 184mg potassium.

Broccoli Egg Casserole

Servings:5
Cooking Time: 3 Hours
Ingredients:
- 4 eggs, beaten
- ½ cup full-fat milk
- 3 tablespoons grass-fed butter, melted
- 1 ½ cup broccoli florets, chopped
- Salt and pepper to taste

Directions:
1. Beat the eggs and milk in a mixing bowl.
2. Grease the bottom of the CrockPot with melted butter.
3. Add in the broccoli florets in the CrockPot and pour the egg mixture.
4. Season with salt and pepper to taste.
5. Close the lid and cook on high for 2 hours or on low for 3 hours.

Nutrition Info:
- Calories per serving: 217; Carbohydrates:4.6 g; Protein: 11.6g; Fat: 16.5g; Sugar: 0.7g; Sodium: 674mg; Fiber: 2.3g

Apricot Butter

Servings:4
Cooking Time: 7 Hours
Ingredients:
- 1 cup apricots, pitted, chopped
- 3 tablespoons butter
- 1 teaspoon ground cinnamon
- 1 teaspoon brown sugar

Directions:
1. Put all ingredients in the Crock Pot and stir well
2. Close the lid and cook them on Low for 7 hours.
3. Then blend the mixture with the help of the immersion blender and cool until cold.

Nutrition Info:
- Per Serving: 99 calories, 0.6g protein, 5.5g carbohydrates, 8.9g fat, 1.1g fiber, 23mg cholesterol, 62mg sodium, 106mg potassium.

Orange Pudding

Servings:4
Cooking Time: 4 Hours
Ingredients:
- 1 cup carrot, grated
- 2 cups of milk
- 1 tablespoon cornstarch
- 1 teaspoon vanilla extract
- ½ teaspoon ground nutmeg

Directions:

1. Put the carrot in the Crock Pot.
2. Add milk, vanilla extract, and ground nutmeg.
3. Then add cornstarch and stir the ingredients until cornstarch is dissolved.
4. Cook the pudding on low for 4 hours.

Nutrition Info:

- Per Serving: 84 calories, 4.3g protein, 10.8g carbohydrates, 2.6g fat, 0.8g fiber, 10mg cholesterol, 77mg sodium, 161mg potassium.

Honey Pumpkin

Servings:4

Cooking Time: 7 Hours

Ingredients:

- 2 tablespoons honey
- 1 tablespoon ground cinnamon
- 1 tablespoon ground cardamom
- 1-pound pumpkin, cubed
- ¼ cup of water

Directions:

1. Put pumpkin in the Crock Pot.
2. Add honey, ground cinnamon, cardamom, and water. Mix the ingredients and close the lid.
3. Cook the pumpkin on Low for 7 hours.

Nutrition Info:

- Per Serving: 79 calories, 1.5g protein, 20.2g carbohydrates, 0.4g fat, 4.6g fiber, 0mg cholesterol, 7mg sodium, 263mg potassium.

Peach Oats

Servings:3

Cooking Time: 7 Hours

Ingredients:

- ½ cup steel cut oats
- 1 cup milk
- ½ cup peaches, pitted, chopped
- 1 teaspoon ground cardamom

Directions:

1. Mix steel-cut oats with milk and pour the mixture in the Crock Pot.
2. Add ground cardamom and peaches. Stir the ingredients gently and close the lid.
3. Cook the meal on low for 7 hours.

Nutrition Info:

- Per Serving: 159 calories, 7g protein, 24.8g carbohydrates, 3.8g fat, 3.2g fiber, 7mg cholesterol, 38mg sodium, 200mg potassium

Carrot Pudding

Servings:4

Cooking Time: 5 Hours

Ingredients:

- 3 cups carrot, shredded
- 1 tablespoon potato starch
- 3 tablespoons maple syrup
- 1 teaspoon ground cinnamon
- 4 cups of milk

Directions:

1. Mix potato starch with milk and pour the liquid in the Crock Pot.
2. Add ground cinnamon, maple syrup, and carrot.
3. Close the lid and cook the pudding on Low for 5 hours.

Nutrition Info:

- Per Serving: 206 calories, 8.7g protein, 33.1g carbohydrates, 5g fat, 2.3g fiber, 20mg cholesterol, 173mg sodium, 437mg potassium

Giant Pancake

Servings:4

Cooking Time: 4 Hours

Ingredients:

- 1 cup pancake mix
- ½ cup milk
- 2 eggs, beaten
- 1 tablespoon coconut oil, melted

Directions:

1. Whisk pancake mix with milk, and eggs.
2. Then brush the Crock Pot mold with coconut oil from inside.
3. Pour the pancake mixture in the Crock Pot and close the lid.
4. Cook it on High for 4 hours.

Nutrition Info:

- Per Serving: 225 calories, 7.8g protein, 29.9g carbohydrates, 8.1g fat, 1g fiber, 94mg cholesterol, 529mg sodium, 7.8mg potassium.

Light Egg Scramble

Servings:2
Cooking Time: 4 Hours
Ingredients:

- 1 tablespoon butter, melted
- 6 eggs, beaten
- 1 teaspoon salt
- 1 teaspoon ground paprika

Directions:

1. Pour the melted butter in the Crock Pot.
2. Add eggs and salt and stir.
3. Cook the eggs on Low for 4 hours. Stir the eggs every 15 minutes.
4. When the egg scramble is cooked, top it with ground paprika.

Nutrition Info:

- Per Serving: 243 calories, 16.8g protein, 1.6g carbohydrates, 19g fat, 0.4g fiber, 506mg cholesterol, 1389mg sodium, 203mg potassium

Salmon Frittata

Servings: 3
Cooking Time: 3 Hours And 40 Minutes
Ingredients:

- 4 eggs, whisked
- ½ teaspoon olive oil
- 2 tablespoons green onions, chopped
- Salt and black pepper to the taste
- 4 ounces smoked salmon, chopped

Directions:

1. Drizzle the oil in your Crock Pot, add eggs, salt and pepper, whisk, cover and cook on Low for 3 hours.
2. Add salmon and green onions, toss a bit, cover, cook on Low for 40 minutes more and divide between plates.
3. Serve right away for breakfast.

Nutrition Info:

- calories 220, fat 10, fiber 2, carbs 15, protein 7

Breakfast Meat Rolls

Servings:12
Cooking Time: 4.5 Hours
Ingredients:

- 1-pound puff pastry
- 1 cup ground pork
- 1 tablespoon garlic, diced
- 1 egg, beaten
- 1 tablespoon sesame oil

Directions:

1. Roll up the puff pastry.
2. Then mix ground pork with garlic and egg.
3. Then spread the puff pastry with ground meat mixture and roll.
4. Cut the puff pastry rolls on small rolls.
5. Then sprinkle the rolls with sesame oil.
6. Arrange the meat rolls in the Crock Pot and close the lid.
7. Cook breakfast on High for 4.5 hours.

Nutrition Info:

- Per Serving: 244 calories, 4.9g protein, 17.3g carbohydrates, 17.2g fat, 0.6g fiber, 20mg cholesterol, 106mg sodium, 31mg potassium.

Crockpot Fisherman's Eggs

Servings:2
Cooking Time: 3 Hours
Ingredients:

- 1 can organic sardines in olive oil
- 2 organic eggs
- ½ cup arugula, rinsed and drained
- ½ of artichoke hearts, chopped
- Salt and pepper to taste

Directions:

1. Put the sardines in the bottom of the CrockPot.
2. Break the eggs on top of the sardines and add the arugula and artichokes on top.
3. Season with salt and pepper to taste.
4. Close the lid and cook on high for 2 hours or on low for 3 hours.

Nutrition Info:

- Calories per serving:315; Carbohydrates: 3.5g; Protein: 28g; Fat:20.6 g; Sugar: 0g; Sodium: 491mg; Fiber: 1.3g

Omelet With Greens

Servings:2
Cooking Time: 2 Hours
Ingredients:

- 3 eggs, beaten
- ¼ cup milk
- 1 cup baby arugula, chopped
- ½ teaspoon salt
- 1 teaspoon avocado oil

Directions:

1. In the bowl mix eggs with milk, salt, and arugula.
2. Then sprinkle the Crock Pot with avocado oil from inside.

3. Pour the omelet egg mixture in the Crock Pot and close the lid.

4. Cook the meal on High for 2 hours.

Nutrition Info:

- Per Serving: 115 calories, 9.6g protein, 2.5g carbohydrates, 7.6g fat, 0.3g fiber, 248mg cholesterol, 691mg sodium, 150mg potassium.

Leek Eggs

Servings:4

Cooking Time: 2.5 Hours

Ingredients:

- 10 oz leek, sliced
- 4 eggs, beaten
- 1 teaspoon olive oil
- ½ teaspoon cumin seeds
- 3 oz Cheddar cheese, shredded

Directions:

1. Mix leek with olive oil and eggs.

2. Then transfer the mixture in the Crock Pot.

3. Sprinkle the egg mixture with Cheddar cheese and cumin seeds.

4. Close the lid and cook the meal on High for 2.5 hours.

Nutrition Info:

- Per Serving: 203 calories, 11.9g protein, 10.8g carbohydrates, 12.9g fat, 1.3g fiber, 186mg cholesterol, 208mg sodium, 212mg potassium

Salami Eggs

Servings:4

Cooking Time: 2.5 Hours

Ingredients:

- 4 oz salami, sliced
- 4 eggs
- 1 teaspoon butter, melted
- 1 tablespoon chives, chopped

Directions:

1. Pour the melted butter in the Crock Pot.

2. Crack the eggs inside.

3. Then top the eggs with salami and chives.

4. Close the lid and cook them on High for 2.5 hours.

Nutrition Info:

- Per Serving: 146 calories, 9.1g protein, 0.9g carbohydrates, 11.6g fat, 0g fiber, 186mg cholesterol, 392mg sodium, 115mg potassium

Baby Carrots In Syrup

Servings:5

Cooking Time: 7 Hours

Ingredients:

- 3 cups baby carrots
- 1 cup apple juice
- 2 tablespoons brown sugar
- 1 teaspoon vanilla extract

Directions:

1. Mix apple juice, brown sugar, and vanilla extract.

2. Pour the liquid in the Crock Pot.

3. Add baby carrots and close the lid.

4. Cook the meal on Low for 7 hours.

Nutrition Info:

- Per Serving: 81 calories, 0g protein, 18.8g carbohydrates, 0.1g fat, 3.7g fiber, 0mg cholesterol, 363mg sodium, 56mg potassium.

Peach, Vanilla And Oats Mix

Servings: 2

Cooking Time: 8 Hours

Ingredients:

- ½ cup steel cut oats
- 2 cups almond milk
- ½ cup peaches, pitted and roughly chopped
- ½ teaspoon vanilla extract
- 1 teaspoon cinnamon powder

Directions:

1. In your Crock Pot, mix the oats with the almond milk, peaches and the other ingredients, toss, put the lid on and cook on Low for 8 hours.

2. Divide into bowls and serve for breakfast right away.

Nutrition Info:

- calories 261, fat 5, fiber 8, carbs 18, protein 6

Creamy Bacon Millet

Servings: 6

Cooking Time: 4 Hrs 10 Minutes

Ingredients:

- 3 cup millet
- 6 cup chicken stock
- 1 tsp salt
- 4 tbsp heavy cream
- 5 oz. bacon, chopped

Directions:

1. Add millet and chicken stock to the Crock Pot.

2. Stir in chopped bacon and salt.

3. Put the cooker's lid on and set the cooking time to 4 hours on High settings.

4. Stir in cream and again cover the lid of the Crock Pot.

5. Cook for 10 minutes on High setting.

6. Serve.

Nutrition Info:

- Per Serving: Calories 572, Total Fat 17.8g, Fiber 9g, Total Carbs 83.09g, Protein 20g

Kale Cups

Servings:4

Cooking Time: 2.5 Hours

Ingredients:

- 1 cup kale, chopped
- 4 eggs, beaten
- 1 teaspoon olive oil
- 1 teaspoon chili powder
- ½ cup Cheddar cheese, shredded

Directions:

1. Mix kale with eggs, olive oil, and chili powder.

2. Transfer the mixture in the ramekins and top with Cheddar cheese.

3. Place the ramekins in the Crock Pot.

4. Close the lid and cook the meal on high for 2.5 hours.

Nutrition Info:

- Per Serving: 140 calories, 9.6g protein, 2.6g carbohydrates, 10.3g fat, 0.5g fiber, 179mg cholesterol, 163mg sodium, 168mg potassium

Bacon Potatoes

Servings:4

Cooking Time: 5 Hours

Ingredients:

- 4 russet potatoes
- 1 teaspoon dried thyme
- 4 teaspoons olive oil
- 4 bacon slices

Directions:

1. Cut the potatoes into halves and sprinkle with dried thyme and olive oil.

2. After this, cut every bacon slice into halves.

3. Put the potatoes in the Crock Pot bowl and top with bacon slices.

4. Close the lid and cook them for 5 hours on High.

Nutrition Info:

- Per Serving: 290 calories, 10.6g protein, 33.9g carbohydrates, 12.8g fat, 5.2g fiber, 21mg cholesterol, 452mg sodium, 976mg potassium.

Chorizo Eggs

Servings:4

Cooking Time: 1.5 Hours

Ingredients:

- 5 oz chorizo, sliced
- 4 eggs, beaten
- 2 oz Parmesan, grated
- 1 teaspoon butter, softened

Directions:

1. Grease the Crock Pot bottom with butter.

2. Add chorizo and cook them on high for 30 minutes.

3. Then flip the sliced chorizo and add eggs and Parmesan.

4. Close the lid and cook the meal on High for 1 hour more.

Nutrition Info:

- Per Serving: 278 calories, 18.6g protein, 1.5g carbohydrates, 21.9g fat, 0g fiber, 208mg cholesterol, 638mg sodium, 200mg potassium

Chocolate Oatmeal

Servings:5

Cooking Time: 4 Hours

Ingredients:

- 1 oz dark chocolate, chopped
- 1 teaspoon vanilla extract
- 2 cups of coconut milk
- 2 cup oatmeal
- ½ teaspoon ground cardamom

Directions:

1. Put all ingredients in the Crock Pot and stir carefully with the help of the spoon.

2. Close the lid and cook the meal for 4 hours on Low.

Nutrition Info:

- Per Serving: 386 calories, 7.1g protein, 32.5g carbohydrates, 27.2g fat, 6.1g fiber,1mg cholesterol, 19mg sodium, 374mg potassium.

Leek Bake

Servings:3

Cooking Time: 8 Hours

Ingredients:

- 2 cups leek, chopped
- 3 oz Cheddar cheese, shredded
- ¼ cup ground chicken
- 1 teaspoon dried thyme
- ½ cup chicken stock

Directions:

1. Pour the chicken stock in the Crock Pot.

2. Put the leek in the chicken stock and sprinkle it with dried thyme and ground chicken.

3. Then top the chicken with Cheddar cheese and close the lid.

4. Cook the leek bake on low for 8 hours.

Nutrition Info:

- Per Serving: 175 calories, 11.5g protein, 9.1g carbohydrates, 10.6g fat, 1.2g fiber, 40mg cholesterol, 325mg sodium, 168mg potassium.

French Breakfast Pudding

Servings: 4

Cooking Time: 1 Hour And 30 Minutes

Ingredients:

- 3 egg yolks
- 6 ounces double cream
- 1 teaspoon vanilla extract
- 2 tablespoons caster sugar

Directions:

1. In a bowl, mix the egg yolks with sugar and whisk well.

2. Add cream and vanilla extract, whisk well, pour into your 4 ramekins, place them in your Crock Pot, add some water to the Crock Pot, cover and cook on High for 1 hour and 30 minutes.

3. Leave aside to cool down and serve.

Nutrition Info:

- calories 261, fat 5, fiber 6, carbs 15, protein 2

Seafood Eggs

Servings:4

Cooking Time: 2.5 Hours

Ingredients:

- 4 eggs, beaten
- 2 tablespoons cream cheese
- 1 teaspoon Italian seasonings
- 6 oz shrimps, peeled
- 1 teaspoon olive oil

Directions:

1. Mix cream cheese with eggs.

2. Add Italian seasonings and shrimps.

3. Then brush the ramekins with olive oil and pour the egg mixture inside.

4. Transfer the ramekins in the Crock Pot.

5. Cook the eggs on High for 2.5 hours.

Nutrition Info:

- Per Serving: 144 calories, 15.6g protein, 1.3g carbohydrates, 8.4g fat, 0g fiber, 260mg cholesterol, 181mg sodium, 138mg potassium

Egg Scramble

Servings:4

Cooking Time: 2.5 Hours

Ingredients:

- 4 eggs, beaten
- 1 tablespoon butter, melted
- 2 oz Cheddar cheese, shredded
- ¼ teaspoon cayenne pepper
- 1 teaspoon ground paprika

Directions:

1. Mix eggs with butter, cheese, cayenne pepper, and ground paprika.

2. Then pour the mixture in the Crock Pot and close the lid.

3. Cook it on high for 2 hours.

4. Then open the lid and scramble the eggs.

5. Close the lid and cook the meal on high for 30 minutes.

Nutrition Info:

- Per Serving: 147 calories, 9.2g protein, 0.9g carbohydrates, 12g fat, 0.2g fiber, 186mg cholesterol, 170mg sodium, 88mg potassium.

Peach Puree

Servings:2

Cooking Time: 7 Hours

Ingredients:

- 2 cups peaches, chopped
- 1 tablespoon sugar
- 1 teaspoon ground cinnamon
- ¼ cup of water

Directions:

1. Put all ingredients in the Crock Pot.

2. Close the lid and cook them on low for 7 hours.

3. Then make the puree with the help of the immersion blender.

4. Store the puree in the fridge for up to 1 day.

Nutrition Info:

- Per Serving: 84 calories, 1.5g protein, 20.9g carbohydrates, 0.4g fat, 2.9g fiber, 0mg cholesterol, 1mg sodium, 290mg potassium

Chicken Omelet

Servings:4
Cooking Time: 3 Hours
Ingredients:
- 4 oz chicken fillet, boiled, shredded
- 1 tomato, chopped
- 4 eggs, beaten
- 1 tablespoon cream cheese
- 1 teaspoon olive oil

Directions:
1. Brush the Crock Pot bowl with olive oil from inside.
2. In the mixing bowl mix shredded chicken, tomato, eggs, and cream cheese.
3. Then pour the mixture in the Crock Pot bowl and close the lid.
4. Cook the omelet for 3 hours on Low.

Nutrition Info:
- Per Serving: 138 calories, 14.1g protein, 1g carbohydrates, 8.5g fat, 0.2g fiber, 192mg cholesterol, 94mg sodium, 168mg potassium.

Sweet Quinoa

Servings:4
Cooking Time: 3 Hours
Ingredients:
- 1 cup quinoa
- ¼ cup dates, chopped
- 3 cups of water
- 1 apricot, chopped
- ½ teaspoon ground nutmeg

Directions:
1. Put quinoa, dates, and apricot in the Crock Pot.
2. Add ground nutmeg and mix the mixture.
3. Cook it on high for 3 hours.

Nutrition Info:
- Per Serving: 194 calories, 6.4g protein, 36.7g carbohydrates, 2.8g fat, 4.1g fiber, 0mg cholesterol, 8g sodium, 338mg potassium.

Milk Pudding

Servings:2
Cooking Time: 7 Hours
Ingredients:
- 1 cup milk
- 3 eggs, beaten
- 2 tablespoons cornstarch
- 1 teaspoon vanilla extract
- 1 tablespoon white sugar

Directions:
1. Mix milk with eggs and cornstarch.
2. Whisk the mixture until smooth and add vanilla extract and white sugar.
3. Pour the liquid in the Crock Pot and close the lid.
4. Cook it on Low for 7 hours.

Nutrition Info:
- Per Serving: 214 calories, 12.3g protein, 20.1g carbohydrates, 9.1g fat, 9.7g fiber, 0.1mg cholesterol, 151mg sodium, 162mg potassium.

Creamy Yogurt

Servings: 8
Cooking Time: 10 Hours
Ingredients:
- 3 teaspoons gelatin
- ½ gallon milk
- 7 ounces plain yogurt
- 1 and ½ tablespoons vanilla extract
- ½ cup maple syrup

Directions:
1. Put the milk in your Crock Pot, cover and cook on Low for 3 hours.
2. In a bowl, mix 1 cup of hot milk from the Crock Pot with the gelatin, whisk well, pour into the Crock Pot, cover and leave aside for 2 hours.
3. Combine 1 cup of milk with the yogurt, whisk really well and pour into the pot.
4. Also add vanilla and maple syrup, stir, cover and cook on Low for 7 more hours.
5. Leave yogurt aside to cool down and serve it for breakfast.

Nutrition Info:
- calories 200, fat 4, fiber 5, carbs 10, protein 5

Coconut Oatmeal

Servings:6
Cooking Time: 5 Hours
Ingredients:
- 2 cups oatmeal
- 2 cups of coconut milk
- 1 cup of water
- 2 tablespoons coconut shred
- 1 tablespoon maple syrup

Directions:
1. Put all ingredients in the Crock Pot and carefully mix.
2. Then close the lid and cook the oatmeal on low for 5 hours.

Nutrition Info:

- Per Serving: 313 calories, 5.4g protein, 25.8g carbohydrates, 22.5g fat, 4.8g fiber, 0mg cholesterol, 16mg sodium, 316mg potassium

Squash Bowls

Servings: 2
Cooking Time: 6 Hours
Ingredients:

- 2 tablespoons walnuts, chopped
- 2 cups squash, peeled and cubed
- ½ cup coconut cream
- ½ teaspoon cinnamon powder
- ½ tablespoon sugar

Directions:

1. In your Crock Pot, mix the squash with the nuts and the other ingredients, toss, put the lid on and cook on Low for 6 hours.
2. Divide into bowls and serve.

Nutrition Info:

- calories 140, fat 1, fiber 2, carbs 2, protein 5

Asparagus Egg Casserole

Servings:4
Cooking Time: 2.5 Hours
Ingredients:

- 7 eggs, beaten
- 4 oz asparagus, chopped, boiled
- 1 oz Parmesan, grated
- 1 teaspoon sesame oil
- 1 teaspoon dried dill

Directions:

1. Pour the sesame oil in the Crock Pot.
2. Then mix dried dill with parmesan, asparagus, and eggs.
3. Pour the egg mixture in the Crock Pot and close the lid.
4. Cook the casserole on high for 2.5 hours.

Nutrition Info:

- Per Serving: 149 calories, 12.6g protein, 2.1g carbohydrates, 10.3g fat, 0.6g fiber, 292mg cholesterol, 175mg sodium, 169mg potassium

Apricot Oatmeal

Servings:4
Cooking Time: 4 Hours
Ingredients:

- 1 ½ cup oatmeal
- 1 cup of water
- 3 cups of milk
- 1 cup apricots, pitted, sliced
- 1 teaspoon butter

Directions:

1. Put oatmeal in the Crock Pot.
2. Add water, milk, and butter.
3. Close the lid and cook the mixture on high for 1 hour.
4. Then add apricots, carefully mix the oatmeal and close the lid.
5. Cook the meal on Low for 3 hours.

Nutrition Info:

- Per Serving: 235 calories, 10.5g protein, 34g carbohydrates, 7g fat, 3.9g fiber, 18mg cholesterol, 97mg sodium, 317mg potassium

Smoked Salmon Omelet

Servings:4
Cooking Time: 2 Hours
Ingredients:

- 4 oz smoked salmon, sliced
- 5 eggs, beaten
- 1 teaspoon ground coriander
- 1 teaspoon butter, melted

Directions:

1. Brush the Crock Pot bottom with melted butter.
2. Then mix eggs with ground coriander and pour the liquid in the Crock Pot.
3. Add smoked salmon and close the lid.
4. Cook the omelet on High for 2 hours.

Nutrition Info:

- Per Serving: 120 calories, 12.1g protein, 0.4g carbohydrates, 7.7g fat, 0g fiber, 214mg cholesterol, 651mg sodium, 124mg potassium

Mocha Latte Quinoa Mix

Servings: 4
Cooking Time: 6 Hours
Ingredients:

- 1 cup hot coffee
- 1 cup quinoa
- 1 cup coconut water
- ¼ cup chocolate chips
- ½ cup coconut cream

Directions:

1. In your Crock Pot, mix quinoa with coffee, coconut water and chocolate chips, cover and cook on Low for 6 hours.
2. Stir, divide into bowls, spread coconut cream all over and serve for breakfast.

Nutrition Info:

- calories 251, fat 4, fiber 7, carbs 15, protein 4

Breakfast Monkey Bread

Servings:6
Cooking Time: 6 Hours
Ingredients:

- 10 oz biscuit rolls
- 1 tablespoon ground cardamom
- 1 tablespoon sugar
- 2 tablespoons coconut oil
- 1 egg, beaten

Directions:

1. Chop the biscuit roll roughly.
2. Mix sugar with ground cardamom.
3. Melt the coconut oil.
4. Put the ½ part of chopped biscuit rolls in the Crock Pot in one layer and sprinkle with melted coconut oil and ½ part of all ground cinnamon mixture.
5. Then top it with remaining biscuit roll chops and sprinkle with cardamom mixture and coconut oil.
6. Then brush the bread with a beaten egg and close the lid.
7. Cook the meal on High for 6 hours.
8. Cook the cooked bread well.

Nutrition Info:

- Per Serving: 178 calories, 6.1g protein, 26.4g carbohydrates, 7g fat, 2g fiber, 27mg cholesterol, 238mg sodium, 21mg potassium.

Squash Butter

Servings:4
Cooking Time: 2 Hours
Ingredients:

- 1 cup butternut squash puree
- 1 teaspoon allspices
- 4 tablespoons applesauce
- 2 tablespoons butter
- 1 teaspoon cornflour

Directions:

1. Put all ingredients in the Crock Pot and mix until homogenous.
2. Then close the lid and cook the butter on High for 2 hours.
3. Transfer the cooked squash butter in the plastic vessel and cool it well.

Nutrition Info:

- Per Serving: 78 calories, 0.2g protein, 6.3g carbohydrates, 5.8g fat, 0.8g fiber, 15mg cholesterol, 44mg sodium, 20mg potassium

Olive Eggs

Servings:4
Cooking Time: 2 Hours
Ingredients:

- 10 kalamata olives, sliced
- 8 eggs, beaten
- 1 teaspoon cayenne pepper
- 1 tablespoon butter

Directions:

1. Grease the Crock Pot bottom with butter.
2. Then add beaten eggs and cayenne pepper.
3. After this, top the eggs with olives and close the lid.
4. Cook the eggs on High for 2 hours.

Nutrition Info:

- Per Serving: 165 calories, 11.2g protein, 1.6g carbohydrates, 12.9g fat, 0.5g fiber, 335mg cholesterol, 240mg sodium, 129mg potassium

Cream Grits

Servings:2
Cooking Time: 5 Hours
Ingredients:

- ½ cup grits
- ½ cup heavy cream
- 1 cup of water
- 1 tablespoon cream cheese

Directions:

1. Put grits, heavy cream, and water in the Crock Pot.
2. Cook the meal on LOW for 5 hours.
3. When the grits are cooked, add cream cheese and stir carefully.
4. Transfer the meal in the serving bowls.

Nutrition Info:

- Per Serving: 151 calories, 1.6g protein, 6.9g carbohydrates, 13.2g fat, 1g fiber, 47mg cholesterol, 116mg sodium, 33mg potassium.

Eggs With Brussel Sprouts

Servings:4
Cooking Time: 6 Hours
Ingredients:

- 1 cup Brussel sprouts, halved
- ½ cup Mozzarella, shredded
- 5 eggs, beaten
- 1 teaspoon chili powder
- 1 teaspoon olive oil

Directions:

1. Pour olive oil in the Crock Pot.
2. Then add the layer of the Brussel sprouts.
3. Sprinkle the vegetables with chili powder and eggs.
4. Then add mozzarella and close the lid.
5. Cook the meal on Low for 6 hours.

Nutrition Info:

- Per Serving: 110 calories, 8.8g protein, 2.9g carbohydrates, 7.5g fat, 1.1g fiber, 206mg cholesterol, 110mg sodium, 172mg potassium

Raisins And Rice Pudding

Servings:4
Cooking Time: 6 Hours
Ingredients:

- 1 cup long-grain rice
- 2.5 cups organic almond milk
- 2 tablespoons cornstarch
- 1 teaspoon vanilla extract
- 2 tablespoons raisins, chopped

Directions:

1. Put all ingredients in the Crock Pot and carefully mix.
2. Then close the lid and cook the pudding for 6 hours on Low.

Nutrition Info:

- Per Serving: 238 calories, 4.1g protein, 49.4g carbohydrates, 1.9g fat, 0.8g fiber, 0mg cholesterol, 91mg sodium, 89mg potassium

Ham Pockets

Servings:4
Cooking Time: 1 Hour
Ingredients:

- 4 pita bread

- ½ cup Cheddar cheese, shredded
- 4 ham slices
- 1 tablespoon mayonnaise
- 1 teaspoon dried dill

Directions:

1. Mix cheese with mayonnaise and dill.
2. Then fill the pita bread with sliced ham and cheese mixture.
3. Wrap the stuffed pitas in the foil and place it in the Crock Pot.
4. Cook them on High for 1 hour.

Nutrition Info:

- Per Serving: 283 calories, 13.7g protein, 35.7g carbohydrates, 9.1g fat, 1.7g fiber, 32mg cholesterol, 801mg sodium, 175mg potassium.

Chia Oatmeal

Servings: 2
Cooking Time: 8 Hours
Ingredients:

- 2 cups almond milk
- 1 cup steel cut oats
- 2 tablespoons butter, soft
- ½ teaspoon almond extract
- 2 tablespoons chia seeds

Directions:

1. In your Crock Pot, mix the oats with the chia seeds and the other ingredients, toss, put the lid on and cook on Low for 8 hours.
2. Stir the oatmeal one more time, divide into 2 bowls and serve.

Nutrition Info:

- calories 812, fat 71.4, fiber 9.4, carbs 41.1, protein 11

Broccoli Omelet

Servings:4
Cooking Time: 2 Hours
Ingredients:

- 5 eggs, beaten
- 1 tablespoon cream cheese
- 3 oz broccoli, chopped
- 1 tomato, chopped
- 1 teaspoon avocado oil

Directions:

1. Mix eggs with cream cheese and transfer in the Crock Pot.
2. Add avocado oil, broccoli, and tomato.

3. Close the lid and cook the omelet on High for 2 hours.

Nutrition Info:

- Per Serving: 99 calories, 7.9g protein, 2.6g carbohydrates, 6.6g fat, 0.8g fiber, 207mg cholesterol, 92mg sodium, 184mg potassium.

Basil Sausages

Servings:5
Cooking Time: 4 Hours
Ingredients:

- 1-pound Italian sausages, chopped
- 1 teaspoon dried basil
- 1 tablespoon olive oil
- 1 teaspoon ground coriander
- ¼ cup of water

Directions:

1. Sprinkle the chopped sausages with ground coriander and dried basil and transfer in the Crock Pot.
2. Add olive oil and water.
3. Close the lid and cook the sausages on high for 4 hours.

Nutrition Info:

- Per Serving: 338 calories, 12.9g protein, 0.6g carbohydrates, 31.2g fat, 0g fiber, 69mg cholesterol, 664mg sodium, 231mg potassium.

Raspberry Chia Porridge

Servings:4
Cooking Time: 4 Hours
Ingredients:

- 1 cup raspberry
- 3 tablespoons maple syrup
- 1 cup chia seeds

- 4 cups of milk

Directions:

1. Put chia seeds and milk in the Crock Pot and cook the mixture on low for 4 hours.
2. Meanwhile, mix raspberries and maple syrup in the blender and blend the mixture until smooth.
3. When the chia porridge is cooked, transfer it in the serving bowls and top with blended raspberry mixture.

Nutrition Info:

- Per Serving: 315 calories, 13.1g protein, 37.7g carbohydrates, 13.9g fat, 11.7g fiber, 20mg cholesterol, 121mg sodium, 332mg potassium

Caramel Pecan Sticky Buns

Servings: 4
Cooking Time: 2 Hours 40 Minutes
Ingredients:

- ¾ cup packed brown sugar
- 15 ounces refrigerated biscuits
- 1 teaspoon ground cinnamon
- 6 tablespoons melted butter
- ¼ cup pecans, finely chopped

Directions:

1. Mix together brown sugar, cinnamon and chopped nuts in a bowl.
2. Dip refrigerator biscuits in melted butter to coat, then in the brown sugar mixture.
3. Grease a crockpot and layer the biscuits in the crock pot.
4. Top with the remaining brown sugar mixture and cover the lid.
5. Cook on HIGH for about 2 hours and dish out to serve.

Nutrition Info:

- Calories: 583 Fat: 23.5g Carbohydrates: 86.2g

Appetizers Recipes

Chipotle Bbq Sausage Bites

Servings: 10
Cooking Time: 2 1/4 Hours
Ingredients:

- 3 pounds small smoked sausages
- 1 cup BBQ sauce
- 2 chipotle peppers in adobo sauce
- 1 tablespoon tomato paste
- 1/4 cup white wine
- Salt and pepper to taste

Directions:

1. Combine all the ingredients in your Crock Pot.
2. Add salt and pepper if needed and cover with a lid.
3. Cook on high settings for 2 hours.
4. Serve the sausage bites warm or chilled.

Bacon Chicken Sliders

Servings: 8
Cooking Time: 4 1/2 Hours
Ingredients:

- 2 pounds ground chicken
- 1 egg
- 1/2 cup breadcrumbs
- 1 shallot, chopped
- Salt and pepper to taste
- 8 bacon slices

Directions:

1. Mix the chicken, egg, breadcrumbs and shallot in a bowl. Add salt and pepper to taste and give it a good mix.
2. Form small sliders then wrap each slider in a bacon slice.
3. Place the sliders in a Crock Pot.
4. Cover with its lid and cook on high settings for 4 hours, making sure to flip them over once during cooking.
5. Serve them warm.

Boiled Peanuts With Skin On

Servings: 8
Cooking Time: 7 1/4 Hours
Ingredients:

- 2 pounds uncooked, whole peanuts
- 1/2 cup salt
- 4 cups water

Directions:

1. Combine all the ingredients in your Crock Pot.
2. Cover and cook on low settings for 7 hours.
3. Drain and allow to cool down before servings.

Maple Syrup Glazed Carrots

Servings: 8
Cooking Time: 6 1/4 Hours
Ingredients:

- 3 pounds baby carrots
- 4 tablespoons butter, melted
- 3 tablespoons maple syrup
- 1/8 teaspoon pumpkin pie spices
- 1 teaspoon salt

Directions:

1. Place the baby carrots in your Crock Pot and add the remaining ingredients.
2. Mix until the carrots are evenly coated.
3. Cover and cook on low settings for 6 hours.
4. Serve the carrots warm or chilled.

Bacon Baked Potatoes

Servings: 8
Cooking Time: 3 1/4 Hours
Ingredients:

- 3 pounds new potatoes, halved
- 8 slices bacon, chopped
- 1 teaspoon dried rosemary
- 1/4 cup chicken stock
- Salt and pepper to taste

Directions:

1. Heat a skillet over medium flame and stir in the bacon. Cook until crisp.
2. Place the potatoes in a Crock Pot. Add the bacon bits and its fat, as well as rosemary, salt and pepper and mix until evenly distributed.
3. Pour in the stock and cook on high heat for 3 hours.
4. Serve the potatoes warm.

Bacon New Potatoes

Servings: 6
Cooking Time: 3 1/4 Hours
Ingredients:

- 3 pounds new potatoes, washed and halved
- 12 slices bacon, chopped
- 2 tablespoons white wine
- Salt and pepper to taste
- 1 rosemary sprig

Directions:

1. Place the potatoes, wine and rosemary in your Crock Pot.
2. Add salt and pepper to taste and top with chopped bacon.
3. Cook on high settings for 3 hours.
4. Serve the potatoes warm.

Cheesy Beef Dip

Servings: 8
Cooking Time: 3 1/4 Hours
Ingredients:

- 2 pounds ground beef
- 1 pound grated Cheddar
- 1/2 cup cream cheese
- 1/2 cup white wine
- 1 poblano pepper, chopped

Directions:

1. Combine all the ingredients in a crock pot.
2. Cook on high settings for 3 hours.
3. Serve preferably warm.

French Onion Dip

Servings: 10
Cooking Time: 4 1/4 Hours
Ingredients:

- 4 large onions, chopped
- 2 tablespoons olive oil
- 1 tablespoon butter
- 1 1/2 cups sour cream
- 1 pinch nutmeg
- Salt and pepper to taste

Directions:

1. Combine the onions, olive oil, butter, salt, pepper and nutmeg in a Crock Pot.
2. Cover and cook on high settings for 4 hours.
3. When done, allow to cool then stir in the sour cream and adjust the taste with salt and pepper.
4. Serve the dip right away.

Sausage Dip

Servings: 8
Cooking Time: 6 1/4 Hours
Ingredients:

- 1 pound fresh pork sausages
- 1 pound spicy pork sausages
- 1 cup cream cheese
- 1 can diced tomatoes
- 2 poblano peppers, chopped

Directions:

1. Combine all the ingredients in a crock pot.
2. Cook on low settings for 6 hours.
3. Serve warm or chilled.

Bourbon Glazed Sausages

Servings: 10
Cooking Time: 4 1/4 Hours
Ingredients:

- 3 pounds small sausage links
- 1/2 cup apricot preserves
- 1/4 cup maple syrup
- 2 tablespoons Bourbon

Directions:

1. Combine all the ingredients in your Crock Pot.
2. Cover with its lid and cook on low settings for 4 hours.

3. Serve the glazed sausages warm or chilled, preferably with cocktail sticks.

Bacon Wrapped Dates

Servings: 8
Cooking Time: 1 3/4 Hours
Ingredients:

- 16 dates, pitted
- 16 almonds
- 16 slices bacon

Directions:

1. Stuff each date with an almond.
2. Wrap each date in bacon and place the wrapped dates in your Crock Pot.
3. Cover with its lid and cook on high settings for 1 1/4 hours.
4. Serve warm or chilled.

Cranberry Baked Brie

Servings: 6
Cooking Time: 2 1/4 Hours
Ingredients:

- 1 wheel of Brie
- 1/2 cup cranberry sauce
- 1/2 teaspoon dried thyme

Directions:

1. Spoon the cranberry sauce in your Crock Pot.
2. Sprinkle with thyme and top with the Brie cheese.
3. Cover with a lid and cook on low settings for 2 hours.
4. The cheese is best served warm with bread sticks or tortilla chips.

Bacon Wrapped Chicken Livers

Servings: 6
Cooking Time: 3 1/2 Hours
Ingredients:

- 2 pounds chicken livers
- Bacon slices as needed

Directions:

1. Wrap each chicken liver in one slice of bacon and place all the livers in your crock pot.
2. Cook on high heat for 3 hours.
3. Serve warm or chilled.

Beef, Pork & Lamb Recipes

Beef Mac&cheese

Servings:4
Cooking Time: 4.5 Hours

Ingredients:

- ½ cup macaroni, cooked
- 10 oz ground beef
- ½ cup marinara sauce
- 1 cup Mozzarella, shredded
- ½ cup of water

Directions:

1. Mix the ground beef with marinara sauce and water and transfer in the Crock Pot.
2. Cook it on High for 4 hours.
3. After this, add macaroni and Mozzarella.
4. Carefully mix the meal and cook it for 30 minutes more on high.

Nutrition Info:

- Per Serving: 218 calories, 25.4g protein, 12.4g carbohydrates, 1.2g fat, 68g fiber, 63mg cholesterol, 219mg sodium, 408mg potassium.

Sour Cream Roast

Servings:4
Cooking Time: 4.5 Hours

Ingredients:

- 1-pound pork shoulder, boneless, chopped
- 1 tablespoon lemon zest, grated
- 4 tablespoons lemon juice
- 1 cup sour cream
- ¼ cup of water

Directions:

1. Sprinkle the pork shoulder with lemon zest and lemon juice.
2. Transfer the meat in the Crock Pot.
3. Add sour cream and water.
4. Close the lid and cook it on high for 5 hours.

Nutrition Info:

- Per Serving: 459 calories, 28.4g protein, 3.1g carbohydrates, 36.4g fat, 0.2g fiber, 127mg cholesterol, 111mg sodium, 480mg potassium

Caribbean Pork Chop

Servings:4
Cooking Time: 10 Hours

Ingredients:

- 1 tablespoon curry powder
- 1 teaspoon cumin
- Salt and pepper to taste
- 1-pound pork loin roast, bones removed
- ½ cup chicken broth

Directions:

1. Place all ingredients in the crockpot. Give a good stir.
2. Close the lid and cook on low for 8 to 10 hours or on high for 7 hours.

Nutrition Info:

- Calories per serving: 471; Carbohydrates: 0.9g; Protein: 43.8g; Fat: 35g; Sugar: 0g; Sodium:528mg; Fiber: 0g

Rosemary Pork

Servings: 4
Cooking Time: 7 Hours

Ingredients:

- 4 pork chops, bone in
- 1 cup chicken stock
- Salt and black pepper to the taste
- 1 teaspoon rosemary, dried
- 3 garlic cloves, minced

Directions:

1. Season pork chops with salt and pepper and place in your Crock Pot.
2. Add rosemary, garlic and stock, cover and cook on Low for 7 hours.
3. Divide pork between plates and drizzle cooking juices all over.

Nutrition Info:

- calories 165, fat 2, fiber 1, carbs 12, protein 26

Hot Beef

Servings:4
Cooking Time: 8 Hours

Ingredients:

- 1-pound beef sirloin, chopped
- 2 tablespoons hot sauce
- 1 tablespoon olive oil
- ½ cup of water

Directions:

1. In the shallow bowl mix hot sauce with olive oil.
2. Then mix beef sirloin with hot sauce mixture and leave for 10 minutes to marinate.

3. Put the marinated beef in the Crock Pot.
4. Add water and close the lid.
5. Cook the meal on Low for 8 hours.

Nutrition Info:

• Per Serving: 241 calories, 34.4g protein, 0.1g carbohydrates, 10.6g fat, 0g fiber, 101mg cholesterol, 266mg sodium, 467mg potassium.

Crockpot Cheeseburgers Casserole

Servings:4
Cooking Time: 8 Hours

Ingredients:

• 1 white onion, chopped
• 1 ½ pounds lean ground beef
• 2 tablespoons mustard
• 1 teaspoon dried basil leaves
• 2 cups cheddar cheese

Directions:

1. Heat skillet over medium flame and sauté both white onions and ground beef for 3 minutes. Continue stirring until lightly brown.
2. Transfer to the crockpot and stir in mustard and basil leaves. Season with salt and pepper.
3. Add cheese on top.
4. Close the lid and cook on low for 8 hours and on high for 6 hours.

Nutrition Info:

• Calories per serving: 472; Carbohydrates: 3g; Protein: 32.7g; Fat: 26.2g; Sugar: 0g; Sodium: 429mg; Fiber: 2.4g

Naked Beef Enchilada In A Crockpot

Servings:4
Cooking Time: 6 Hours

Ingredients:

• 1-pound ground beef
• 2 tablespoons enchilada spice mix
• 1 cup cauliflower florets
• 2 cups Mexican cheese blend, grated
• ¼ cup cilantro, chopped

Directions:

1. In a skillet, sauté the ground beef over medium flame for 3 minutes.
2. Transfer to the crockpot and add the enchilada spice mix and cauliflower.
3. Stir to combine.
4. Add the Mexican cheese blend on top.
5. Cook on low for 6 hours or on high for 4 hours.

6. Sprinkle with cilantro on top.

Nutrition Info:

• Calories per serving: 481; Carbohydrates: 1g; Protein: 35.1g; Fat: 29.4g; Sugar: 0g; Sodium: 536mg; Fiber:0 g

Bbq Beer Beef Tenderloin

Servings:4
Cooking Time: 10 Hours

Ingredients:

• ¼ cup beer
• 1-pound beef tenderloin
• ½ cup BBQ sauce
• 1 teaspoon fennel seeds
• 1 teaspoon olive oil

Directions:

1. Mix BBQ sauce with beer, fennel seeds, and olive oil.
2. Pour the liquid in the Crock Pot.
3. Add beef tenderloin and close the lid.
4. Cook the meal on Low for 10 hours.

Nutrition Info:

• Per Serving: 299 calories, 33g protein, 12.1g carbohydrates, 11.7g fat, 0.4g fiber, 104mg cholesterol, 418mg sodium, 482mg potassium.

Pork With Apples

Servings: 4
Cooking Time: 8 Hrs.

Ingredients:

• A pinch of nutmeg, ground
• 2 lbs. pork tenderloin
• 4 apples, cored and sliced
• 2 tbsp maple syrup

Directions:

1. Add apples to the insert of the Crock Pot.
2. Drizzle nutmeg over the apples then add pork along with remaining ingredients.
3. Put the cooker's lid on and set the cooking time to 8 hours on Low settings.
4. Slice the pork and return to the apple mixture.
5. Mix well and serve warm.

Nutrition Info:

• Per Serving: Calories: 400, Total Fat: 4g, Fiber: 5g, Total Carbs: 12g, Protein: 20g

Taco Pork

Servings:5
Cooking Time: 5 Hours
Ingredients:
- 1-pound pork shoulder, chopped
- 1 tablespoon taco seasonings
- 1 tablespoon lemon juice
- 1 cup of water

Directions:
1. Mix pork shoulder with taco seasonings and place in the Crock Pot.
2. Add water and cook it on High for 5 hours.
3. After this, transfer the cooked meat in the bowl and shred gently with the help of the fork.
4. Add lemon juice and shake gently.

Nutrition Info:
- Per Serving: 274 calories, 21.1g protein, 1.7g carbohydrates, 19.4g fat, 0g fiber, 82mg cholesterol, 232mg sodium, 303mg potassium

Sweet Beef

Servings:4
Cooking Time: 5 Hours
Ingredients:
- 1-pound beef roast, sliced
- 1 tablespoon maple syrup
- 2 tablespoons lemon juice
- 1 teaspoon dried oregano
- 1 cup of water

Directions:
1. Mix water with maple syrup, lemon juice, and dried oregano.
2. Then pour the liquid in the Crock Pot.
3. Add beef roast and close the lid.
4. Cook the meal on High for 5 hours.

Nutrition Info:
- Per Serving: 227 calories, 34.5g protein, 3.8g carbohydrates, 7.2g fat, 0.2g fiber, 101mg cholesterol, 78mg sodium, 483mg potassium.

Beef Brisket In Orange Juice

Servings:4
Cooking Time: 5 Hours
Ingredients:
- 1 cup of orange juice
- 2 cups of water
- 2 tablespoons butter
- 12 oz beef brisket
- ½ teaspoon salt

Directions:
1. Toss butter in the skillet and melt.
2. Put the beef brisket in the melted butter and roast on high heat for 3 minutes per side.
3. Then sprinkle the meat with salt and transfer in the Crock Pot.
4. Add orange juice and water.
5. Close the lid and cook the meat on High for 5 hours.

Nutrition Info:
- Per Serving: 237 calories, 26.3g protein, 6.5g carbohydrates, 11.2g fat, 0.1g fiber, 91mg cholesterol, 392mg sodium, 470mg potassium.

Pan "grilled" Flank Steak

Servings:4
Cooking Time: 10 Hours
Ingredients:
- 1 ½ pounds flank steak, fat trimmed
- Salt and pepper to taste
- A pinch of rosemary
- 1 tablespoon butter, melted
- 1 tablespoon parsley, chopped

Directions:
1. Season the flank steak with salt and pepper to taste.
2. Rub with a pinch of rosemary.
3. Pour the butter in the crockpot and add the slices of flank steak.
4. Close the lid and cook on low for 10 hours or on high for 8 hours.
5. Garnish with parsley before serving.

Nutrition Info:
- Calories per serving: 397; Carbohydrates: 1g; Protein:26.3 g; Fat: 20.7g; Sugar: 0g; Sodium:644mg; Fiber: 0.3g

Basil Beef

Servings:4
Cooking Time: 4 Hours
Ingredients:
- 1-pound beef loin, chopped
- 2 tablespoons dried basil
- 2 tablespoons butter
- ½ cup of water
- 1 teaspoon salt

Directions:
1. Toss the butter in the skillet and melt it.
2. Then mix the beef loin with dried basil and put in the hot butter.

3. Roast the meat for 2 minutes per side and transfer in the Crock Pot.

4. Add salt and water.

5. Close the lid and cook the beef on high for 4 hours.

Nutrition Info:

• Per Serving: 220 calories, 21g protein, 1.4g carbohydrates, 13.9g fat, 0g fiber, 76mg cholesterol, 1123mg sodium, 6mg potassium.

Apple Pork

Servings:4

Cooking Time: 8 Hours

Ingredients:

• 1-pound pork tenderloin, chopped

• 1 teaspoon ground cinnamon

• 1 tablespoon maple syrup

• 1 cup apples, chopped

• 1 cup of water

Directions:

1. Mix apples with ground cinnamon and put in the Crock Pot.

2. Add water, maple syrup, and pork tenderloin.

3. Close the lid and cook the meal on Low for 8 hours.

Nutrition Info:

• Per Serving: 206 calories, 29.9g protein, 11.5g carbohydrates, 4.1g fat, 1.7g fiber, 83mg cholesterol, 67mg sodium, 550mg potassium

Honey Beef Sausages

Servings:4

Cooking Time: 4.5 Hours

Ingredients:

• 1-pound beef sausages

• 2 tablespoons of liquid honey

• 1 teaspoon dried dill

• ½ teaspoon salt

• ¼ cup heavy cream

Directions:

1. In the mixing bowl mix liquid honey with dried dill and salt.

2. Then add cream and whisk until smooth.

3. Pour the liquid in the Crock Pot.

4. Add beef sausages and close the lid.

5. Cook the meal on High for 4.5 hours.

Nutrition Info:

• Per Serving: 507 calories, 15.9g protein, 12.1g carbohydrates, 43.9g fat, 0.1g fiber, 91mg cholesterol, 1207mg sodium, 234mg potassium.

Simple Pork Chop Casserole

Servings:4

Cooking Time: 10 Hours

Ingredients:

• 4 pork chops, bones removed and cut into bite-sized pieces

• 3 tablespoons minced onion

• ½ cup water

• Salt and pepper to taste

• 1 cup heavy cream

Directions:

1. Place the pork chop slices, onions, and water in the crockpot.

2. Season with salt and pepper to taste.

3. Close the lid and cook on low for 10 hours or on high for 8 hours.

4. Halfway through the cooking time, pour in the heavy cream.

Nutrition Info:

• Calories per serving: 515; Carbohydrates: 2.5g; Protein: 39.2g; Fat: 34.3g; Sugar: 0g; Sodium: 613mg; Fiber:0.9 g

Rosemary And Bacon Pork Chops

Servings:4

Cooking Time: 4 Hours

Ingredients:

• 4 pork chops

• 4 bacon slices

• 1 teaspoon dried rosemary

• 1 tablespoon olive oil

• ½ cup of water

Directions:

1. Rub the pork chops with rosemary and olive oil.

2. Then wrap the pork chops in the bacon and put in the hot skillet.

3. Roast the pork chops for 1 minute per side.

4. Then transfer them in the Crock Pot. Add water.

5. Close the lid and cook the meat on High for 4 hours.

Nutrition Info:

• Per Serving: 390 calories, 25g protein, 0.5g carbohydrates, 31.4g fat, 0.1g fiber, 90mg cholesterol, 496mg sodium, 386mg potassium

Crockpot Pork Adobo

Servings:2
Cooking Time: 12 Hours
Ingredients:
- ¼ cup Soy Sauce
- 4 tablespoons apple cider vinegar
- 1-pound pork loin, chopped
- 1 bay leaf
- 1 teaspoon whole peppercorns

Directions:
1. Place all ingredients in the crockpot.
2. Give a good stir to combine all ingredients.
3. Cook on low for 12 hours or on high for 8 hours.

Nutrition Info:
- Calories per serving: 328; Carbohydrates: 3.21g; Protein: 53.84g; Fat: 9.38g; Sugar: 0.29g; Sodium: 1261mg; Fiber: 0.7g

Roast And Pepperoncinis

Servings: 4
Cooking Time: 8 Hours
Ingredients:
- 5 pounds beef chuck roast
- 1 tablespoon soy sauce
- 10 pepperoncinis
- 1 cup beef stock
- 2 tablespoons butter, melted

Directions:
1. In your Crock Pot, mix beef roast with soy sauce, pepperoncinis, stock and butter, toss well, cover and cook on Low for 8 hours.
2. Transfer roast to a cutting board, shred using2 forks, return to Crock Pot, toss, divide between plates and serve.

Nutrition Info:
- calories 362, fat 4, fiber 8, carbs 17, protein 17

Crockpot Beef And Broccoli

Servings:2
Cooking Time: 12 Hours
Ingredients:
- ½ stick butter
- 2 tablespoons garlic, minced
- 2 cups stir fry beef
- 1 broccoli head, cut into florets
- ½ cup parmesan cheese, grated

Directions:

1. Heat oil in a skillet over medium flame and sauté the garlic until fragrant and lightly brown.
2. Add the beef and stir fry for 3 minutes. Stir constantly.
3. Transfer to the crockpot and add the broccoli florets. Season with salt and pepper to taste.
4. Add a few tablespoons of water.
5. Pour the parmesan cheese on top.
6. Close the lid and cook on low for 12 hours or on high for 9 hours.

Nutrition Info:
- Calories per serving: 427; Carbohydrates: 0.9g; Protein: 34.2g; Fat: 32.7g; Sugar: 0g; Sodium:617 mg; Fiber: 0g

Easy Pork Chop Dinner

Servings:4
Cooking Time: 10 Hours
Ingredients:
- 2 teaspoons olive oil
- 2 cloves of garlic, chopped
- 1 onion, chopped
- 4 pork cops
- 2 cups chicken broth

Directions:
1. In a skillet, heat the oil and sauté the garlic and onions until fragrant and lightly golden. Add in the pork chops and cook for 2 minutes for 2 minutes on each side.
2. Pour the chicken broth and scrape the bottom to remove the browning.
3. Transfer to the crockpot. Season with salt and pepper to taste.
4. Close the lid and cook on low for 10 hours or on high for 7 hours.

Nutrition Info:
- Calories per serving: 481; Carbohydrates: 2.5g; Protein: 38.1g; Fat: 30.5g; Sugar: 0.3g; Sodium: 735mg; Fiber: 1.2g

3-ingredients Beef Roast

Servings:6
Cooking Time: 5 Hours
Ingredients:
- 2-pounds beef chuck roast, chopped
- 1 teaspoon ground cumin
- 1 cup of water

Directions:
1. Put all ingredients from the list above in the Crock Pot.
2. Close the lid and cook the meal on High for 5 hours.

Nutrition Info:
- Per Serving: 550 calories, 39.6g protein, 0.2g carbohydrates, 42.1g fat, 0g fiber, 156mg cholesterol, 99mg sodium, 351mg potassium.

Horseradish Pork Chops

Servings:4
Cooking Time: 5 Hours
Ingredients:
- 4 pork chops
- 5 tablespoons horseradish
- ½ cup of water
- 1 onion, sliced
- 1 tablespoon avocado oil

Directions:
1. Mix avocado oil with horseradish and rub the pork chops/
2. Put the pork chops and all remaining horseradish mixture in the Crock Pot.
3. Add onion and water.
4. Cook the pork chops on high for 5 hours.

Nutrition Info:
- Per Serving: 281 calories, 18.5g protein, 4.9g carbohydrates, 20.5g fat, 1.4g fiber, 69mg cholesterol, 117mg sodium, 373mg potassium

Beef Sausages In Maple Syrup

Servings:4
Cooking Time: 5 Hours
Ingredients:
- 1-pound beef sausages
- ½ cup maple syrup
- 3 tablespoons butter
- 1 teaspoon ground cumin
- ¼ cup of water

Directions:
1. Toss butter in the skillet and melt it.
2. Then pour the melted butter in the Crock Pot.

3. Add water, cumin, and maple syrup. Stir the liquid until smooth.
4. Add beef sausages and close the lid.
5. Cook the meal on High for 5 hours.

Nutrition Info:
- Per Serving: 630 calories, 15.8 g protein, 29.7g carbohydrates, 50g fat, 0.1g fiber, 103mg cholesterol, 979mg sodium, 307mg potassium.

Fennel Seeds Pork Chops

Servings:4
Cooking Time: 6 Hours
Ingredients:
- 4 pork chops
- 1 tablespoon fennel seeds
- 3 tablespoons avocado oil
- 1 teaspoon garlic, diced
- ½ cup of water

Directions:
1. Mix fennel seeds with avocado oil and garlic. Mash the mixture.
2. Then rub the pork chops with fennel seeds mixture and transfer in the Crock Pot.
3. Add water and close the lid.
4. Cook the meat on low for 6 hours.

Nutrition Info:
- Per Serving: 276 calories, 18.4g protein, 1.6g carbohydrates, 21.4g fat, 1.1g fiber, 69mg cholesterol, 59mg sodium, 336mg potassium

Beef Pot Roast

Servings:6
Cooking Time: 12 Hours
Ingredients:
- 2 pounds shoulder pot roast, bones removed
- Salt and pepper to taste
- ¼ cup water
- 1 package mushrooms, sliced
- 1 tablespoon Worcestershire sauce

Directions:
1. Place all ingredients in the crockpot.
2. Give a good stir.
3. Close the lid and cook on low for 12 hours or on high for 10 hours.

Nutrition Info:
- Calories per serving: 419; Carbohydrates:3 g; Protein: 32.6g; Fat: 29.6g; Sugar: 0.7g; Sodium: 513mg; Fiber: 1.4g

Braised Ham

Servings:4
Cooking Time: 10 Hours
Ingredients:
- 12 oz smoked shoulder ham
- 1 tablespoon mustard
- 2 cups of water
- ¼ cup maple syrup
- ¼ cup beer

Directions:
1. Rub the smoked shoulder ham with mustard and transfer in the Crock Pot.
2. Add water and beer.
3. Close the lid and cook the ham on low for 10 hours.
4. When the time is finished, sprinkle the meat with maple syrup and slice.

Nutrition Info:
- Per Serving: 221 calories, 15.7g protein, 15.7g carbohydrates, 9.9g fat, 0.4g fiber, 50mg cholesterol, 747mg sodium, 64mg potassium

Skirt Steak With Red Pepper Sauce

Servings:4
Cooking Time: 12 Hours
Ingredients:
- 2 red bell peppers, chopped
- 2 tablespoons olive oil
- 1 teaspoon thyme leaves
- 1-pound skirt steak, sliced into 1 inch thick
- Salt and pepper to taste

Directions:
1. In a food processor, mix together the red bell peppers, olive oil, and thyme leaves. Blend until smooth. Add water to make the mixture slightly runny. Set aside.
2. Season the skirt steak with salt and pepper.
3. Place in the crockpot and pour over the pepper sauce.
4. Add more salt and pepper if desired.
5. Close the lid and cook on low for 12 hours or on high for 10 hours.

Nutrition Info:
- Calories per serving: 396; Carbohydrates:4 g; Protein: 32.5g; Fat: 21g; Sugar: 0g; Sodium: 428mg; Fiber: 2.8g

Filet Mignon With Fresh Basil Rub

Servings:4
Cooking Time: 7 Hours

Ingredients:
- 1 ½ teaspoon fresh basil, minced
- 1 ½ teaspoon thyme, minced
- 2 teaspoons garlic, minced
- Salt and pepper to taste
- 4 beef tenderloin steaks, cut to 1-inch thick

Directions:
1. Line the bottom of the crockpot with foil.
2. In a mixing bowl, combine the basil, thyme, and garlic. Season with salt and pepper.
3. Rub the steaks with the spice rub. Allow to marinate for at least 30 minutes.
4. Place inside the crockpot and cook on high for 7 hours or on low for 10 hours.

Nutrition Info:
- Calories per serving: 424; Carbohydrates: 2.4g; Protein: 30.6g; Fat: 26.3g; Sugar: 0g; Sodium: 537mg; Fiber: 0.8g

Roast With Pepperoncini

Servings: 4
Cooking Time: 8 Hrs.
Ingredients:
- 5 lbs. beef chuck roast
- 1 tbsp soy sauce
- 10 pepperoncini's
- 1 cup beef stock
- 2 tbsp butter, melted

Directions:
1. Add beef roast and all other ingredients to the insert of Crock Pot.
2. Put the cooker's lid on and set the cooking time to 8 hours on Low settings.
3. Shred the cooked meat with the help of 2 forks and return to the cooker.
4. Mix gently and serve warm.

Nutrition Info:
- Per Serving: Calories: 362, Total Fat: 4g, Fiber: 8g, Total Carbs: 17g, Protein: 17g

One Pot Pork Chops

Servings:6
Cooking Time: 10 Hours
Ingredients:

- 6 pork chops
- 2 cups broccoli florets
- ½ cup green and red bell peppers
- 1 onion, sliced
- Salt and pepper to taste

Directions:

1. Place all ingredients in the crockpot.
2. Give a stir to mix everything.
3. Close the lid and cook on low for 10 hours or on high for 8 hours.

Nutrition Info:

- Calories per serving: 496; Carbohydrates: 6g; Protein: 37.1g; Fat: 23.7g; Sugar: 0.8g; Sodium: 563mg; Fiber: 4.3g

Kebab Cubes

Servings:4
Cooking Time: 5 Hours
Ingredients:

- 1 teaspoon curry powder
- 1 teaspoon dried mint
- 1 teaspoon cayenne pepper
- ½ cup plain yogurt
- 1-pound beef tenderloin, cubed

Directions:

1. In the mixing bowl, mix beef cubes with plain yogurt, cayenne pepper, dried mint, and curry powder.
2. Then put the mixture in the Crock Pot. Add water if there is not enough liquid and close the lid.
3. Cook the meal on High for 5 hours.

Nutrition Info:

- Per Serving: 259 calories, 34.7g protein, 2.7g carbohydrates, 10.9g fat, 0.3g fiber, 106mg cholesterol, 89mg sodium, 495mg potassium.

Succulent Pork Ribs

Servings:4
Cooking Time: 8 Hours
Ingredients:

- 12 oz pork ribs, roughly chopped
- ¼ cup of orange juice
- 1 cup of water
- 1 teaspoon ground nutmeg
- 1 teaspoon salt

Directions:

1. Pour water and orange juice in the Crock Pot.
2. Then sprinkle the pork ribs with ground nutmeg and salt.
3. Put the pork ribs in the Crock Pot and close the lid.
4. Cook the meat on low for 8 hours.

Nutrition Info:

- Per Serving: 242 calories, 22.7g protein, 1.9g carbohydrates, 15.3g fat, 0.1g fiber, 88mg cholesterol, 633mg sodium, 279mg potassium

Citrus-rubbed Skirt Steak

Servings:5
Cooking Time: 12 Hours
Ingredients:

- 2 teaspoons grated lemon rind
- 2 teaspoons grated orange rind
- Salt and pepper to taste
- 1 clove of garlic, minced
- 1-pound skirt steak

Directions:

1. Line the bottom of the crockpot with foil.
2. In a bowl, mix the lemon rind, orange rind, salt, pepper, and garlic.
3. Rub the spice mix onto the skirt steak.
4. Place inside the crockpot and cook on low for 10 hours or on high for 7 hours.

Nutrition Info:

- Calories per serving: 362; Carbohydrates: 2.3g; Protein: 32.6g; Fat: 15.2g; Sugar: 0g; Sodium: 471mg; Fiber:1.6 g

Old Fashioned Shredded Beef

Servings:4
Cooking Time: 6 Hours
Ingredients:

- ½ cup of canned soup
- 1 cup of water
- 1-pound beef tenderloin
- 1 teaspoon peppercorns

Directions:

1. Pour water in the Crock Pot.
2. Add peppercorns and beef tenderloin.
3. Close the lid and cook the meat on High for 5 hours.
4. After this, drain water and shred the meat with the help of the forks.
5. Add canned soup and stir well.
6. Cook the beef on High for 1 hour.

Nutrition Info:

- Per Serving: 247 calories, 33.4g protein, 1.8g carbohydrates, 10.9g fat, 0.1g fiber, 106mg cholesterol, 291mg sodium, 427mg potassium.

Cajun Pork Loin

Servings:3
Cooking Time: 7 Hours
Ingredients:
- 12 oz pork loin
- 1 tablespoon Cajun seasonings
- 2 tablespoons sunflower oil
- ½ cup of water
- 3 garlic cloves, sliced

Directions:
1. Rub the pork loin with Cajun seasonings and sprinkle with sunflower oil.
2. Transfer the meat in the Crock Pot.
3. Add water and garlic cloves.
4. Close the lid and cook the meat on low for 7 hours.

Nutrition Info:
- Per Serving: 361 calories, 31.2g protein, 1g carbohydrates, 25.1g fat, 0.1g fiber, 91mg cholesterol, 122mg sodium, 492mg potassium

Sweet Lamb Ribs

Servings:3
Cooking Time: 9 Hours
Ingredients:
- 8 oz lamb ribs, chopped
- 1 teaspoon tomato paste
- 2 teaspoons liquid honey
- ½ cup butter
- ¼ cup of water

Directions:
1. Rub the lamb ribs with tomato paste and liquid honey.
2. Then place them in the Crock Pot.
3. Add butter and water.
4. Close the lid and cook the meat on low for 9 hours.

Nutrition Info:
- Per Serving: 414 calories, 15.8g protein, 4.2g carbohydrates, 37.4g fat, 0.1g fiber, 132mg cholesterol, 274mg sodium, 30mg potassium.

Beer Sausages

Servings:4
Cooking Time: 7 Hours
Ingredients:
- 1-pound beef sausages

- 3 tablespoons butter
- 1 teaspoon ground black pepper
- 1 teaspoon salt
- 1 cup beer

Directions:
1. Toss the butter in the skillet and melt it.
2. Add beef sausages and roast them on high heat for 2 minutes per side.
3. Transfer the beef sausages in the Crock Pot.
4. Add ground black pepper, salt, and beer.
5. Close the lid and cook the meal on Low for 7 hours.

Nutrition Info:
- Per Serving: 552 calories, 16.1g protein, 5.5g carbohydrates, 49.8g fat, 0.1g fiber, 103mg cholesterol, 1558mg sodium, 240mg potassium.

Tenderloin Steaks With Red Wine And Mushrooms

Servings:4
Cooking Time: 12 Hours
Ingredients:
- 4 pounds beef tenderloin steaks
- Salt and pepper to taste
- 1 package Portobello mushrooms, sliced
- 1 cup dry red wine
- 2 tablespoons butter

Directions:
1. Place all ingredients in the crockpot.
2. Give a good stir.
3. Close the lid and cook on low for 12 hours or on high for 10 hours.

Nutrition Info:
- Calories per serving: 415; Carbohydrates:7.2 g; Protein:30.3 g; Fat: 27.4g; Sugar: 0g; Sodium: 426mg; Fiber:3.8 g

Chili Crockpot Brisket

Servings:4
Cooking Time: 12 Hours
Ingredients:
- 4 pounds beef brisket
- 1 bottle chili sauce
- Salt and pepper to taste
- 1 cup onion, chopped
- 1/8 cup water

Directions:
1. Place all ingredients in the crockpot.
2. Give a good stir.

3. Close the lid and cook on low for 12 hours or on high for 10 hours.

Nutrition Info:

- Calories per serving: 634; Carbohydrates: 2.1g; Protein: 30.2g; Fat: 45.4g; Sugar:0 g; Sodium: 835mg; Fiber: 1.4g

Roasted Beef Tenderloin

Servings:5

Cooking Time: 12 Hours

Ingredients:

- 3 ½ pounds beef tenderloin
- Salt and pepper to taste
- 1 teaspoon dry mustard
- 3 tablespoons unsalted butter
- 2 cloves of garlic, minced

Directions:

1. Line the bottom of the crockpot with foil.
2. Season the beef tenderloin with salt and pepper. Rub the dry mustard.
3. In a skillet, heat the butter over medium flame. Sauté the garlic until lightly brown and fragrant.
4. Sear the beef tenderloin in the skillet for 2 minutes on each side.
5. Place in the crockpot.
6. Close the lid and cook on low for 12 hours or on high for 9 hours.

Nutrition Info:

- Calories per serving: 473; Carbohydrates: 0.7g; Protein: 32.5g; Fat: 24.1g; Sugar: 0g; Sodium: 527mg; Fiber: 0g

Pork Tenderloin And Apples

Servings: 4

Cooking Time: 8 Hours

Ingredients:

- A pinch of nutmeg, ground
- 2 pounds pork tenderloin
- 4 apples, cored and sliced
- 2 tablespoons maple syrup

Directions:

1. Place apples in your Crock Pot, sprinkle nutmeg over them, add pork tenderloin, sprinkle some more nutmeg, drizzle the maple syrup, cover and cook on Low for 8 hours.
2. Slice pork tenderloin, divide it between plates and serve with apple slices and cooking juices.

Nutrition Info:

- calories 400, fat 4, fiber 5, carbs 12, protein 20

Sweet Pork Shoulder

Servings:2

Cooking Time: 8 Hours

Ingredients:

- 8 oz pork shoulder
- 3 tablespoons agave syrup
- 1 tablespoon sunflower oil
- ½ cup of water

Directions:

1. Brush the pork shoulder with sunflower oil and agave syrup.
2. Put it in the Crock Pot. Add water.
3. Cook the meat on low for 8 hours.

Nutrition Info:

- Per Serving: 489 calories, 26.4g protein, 25.2g carbohydrates, 31.3g fat, 0g fiber, 102mg cholesterol, 100mg sodium, 393mg potassium

Spiced Beef

Servings:4

Cooking Time: 9 Hours

Ingredients:

- 1-pound beef loin
- 1 teaspoon allspice
- 1 teaspoon olive oil
- 1 tablespoon minced onion
- 1 cup of water

Directions:

1. Rub the beef loin with allspice, olive oil, and minced onion.
2. Put the meat in the Crock Pot.
3. Add water and close the lid.
4. Cook the beef on Low for 9 hours.
5. When the meat is cooked, slice it into servings.

Nutrition Info:

- Per Serving: 219 calories, 30.4g protein, 0.6g carbohydrates, 10.7g fat, 0.2g fiber, 81mg cholesterol, 65mg sodium, 395mg potassium.

Smothered Pepper Steak

Servings:4

Cooking Time: 10 Hours

Ingredients:

- 1 can diced tomatoes
- 1 package bell peppers
- Salt and pepper to taste
- 1 tablespoon soy sauce
- 4 sirloin patties

Directions:

1. Place the diced tomatoes (juices and all) in the crockpot.
2. Add the bell peppers. Season with salt, pepper, and soy sauce.
3. Arrange the sirloin patties on top.
4. Close the lid and cook on low for 10 hours or on high for 7 hours.

Nutrition Info:
- Calories per serving: 387; Carbohydrates: 5g; Protein: 24.1g; Fat: 18.5g; Sugar: 0.8g; Sodium: 462mg; Fiber: 2.7g

Shredded Pork

Servings:4
Cooking Time: 5 Hours
Ingredients:
- 10 oz pork loin
- ½ cup cream
- 1 cup of water
- 1 teaspoon coriander seeds
- 1 teaspoon salt

Directions:
1. Put all ingredients in the Crock Pot.
2. Cook it on High for 5 hours.
3. Then open the lid and shredded pork with the help of 2 forks.

Nutrition Info:
- Per Serving: 191 calories, 19.6g protein, 0.9g carbohydrates, 11.5g fat, 0g fiber, 62mg cholesterol, 367mg sodium, 312mg potassium

Dijon Basil Pork Loin

Servings:4
Cooking Time: 10 Hours
Ingredients:
- 1 pork loin roast, trimmed from excess fat
- 2 tablespoons Dijon mustard
- 1 teaspoon marjoram
- Salt and pepper to taste
- ¼ cup basil, chopped

Directions:
1. Rub the pork loin roast with mustard, marjoram, salt and pepper.
2. Use your hands to massage the pork.
3. Place in the crockpot and sprinkle with chopped basil.
4. Close the lid and cook on low for 10 hours or on high for 8 hours.

Nutrition Info:
- Calories per serving: 449; Carbohydrates: 3g; Protein: 38.2g; Fat:33.1g; Sugar:0 g; Sodium: 764mg; Fiber: 1.3g

Cayenne Pepper Strips

Servings:4
Cooking Time: 4 Hours
Ingredients:
- 1-pound pork sirloin, cut into strips
- 1 teaspoon cayenne pepper
- 2 tablespoons ketchup
- 1 tablespoon avocado oil
- 1 cup of water

Directions:
1. Mix ketchup with cayenne pepper and avocado oil.
2. Then carefully brush the pork strips with ketchup mixture and put in the Crock Pot.
3. Add water and close the lid.
4. Cook the meat on high for 4 hours.

Nutrition Info:
- Per Serving: 204 calories, 23.3g protein, 2.3g carbohydrates, 10.6g fat, 0.3g fiber, 80mg cholesterol, 151mg sodium, 49mg potassium

Bacon Swiss Pork Chops

Servings:8
Cooking Time: 10 Hours
Ingredients:
- 8 pork chops, bone in
- 2 tablespoons olive oil
- 4 cloves of garlic
- 12 bacon strips, cut in half
- 1 cup Swiss cheese, shredded

Directions:
1. Season the pork chops with salt and pepper to taste
2. In a skillet, heat the olive oil over medium flame and sauté the garlic until fragrant and slightly golden.
3. Transfer to the crockpot.
4. Wrap the bacon strips around the pork chops.
5. Place in the crockpot and sprinkle with shredded Swiss cheese.
6. Close the lid and cook on low for 10 hours or on high for 8 hours.

Nutrition Info:
- Calories per serving: 519; Carbohydrates: 0.5g; Protein: 42.3g; Fat: 40.2g; Sugar: 0g; Sodium: 732mg; Fiber: 0g

Poultry Recipes

Sun-dried Tomato Chicken

Servings:10

Cooking Time: 8 Hours

Ingredients:

* 1 tablespoon butter
* 3 cloves of garlic, minced
* 4 pounds whole chicken, cut into pieces
* 1 cup sun-dried tomatoes in vinaigrette
* Salt and pepper to taste

Directions:

1. In a skillet, melt the butter and sauté the garlic until lightly browned.
2. Add the chicken pieces and cook for 3 minutes until slightly browned.
3. Transfer to the crockpot and stir in the sun-dried tomatoes including the vinaigrette.
4. Season with salt and pepper to taste.
5. Close the lid and cook on low for 8 hours or on high for 6 hours.

Nutrition Info:

* Calories per serving: 397; Carbohydrates:9.4 g; Protein: 30.26g; Fat:14.1 g; Sugar: 0.4g; Sodium: 472mg; Fiber: 5.8g

Chicken Stuffed With Plums

Servings:6

Cooking Time: 4 Hours

Ingredients:

* 6 chicken fillets
* 1 cup plums, pitted, sliced
* 1 cup of water
* 1 teaspoon salt
* 1 teaspoon white pepper

Directions:

1. Beat the chicken fillets gently and rub with salt and white pepper.
2. Then put the sliced plums on the chicken fillets and roll them.
3. Secure the chicken rolls with toothpicks and put in the Crock Pot.
4. Add water and close the lid.
5. Cook the meal on High for 4 hours.
6. Then remove the chicken from the Crock Pot, remove the toothpicks and transfer in the serving plates.

Nutrition Info:

* Per Serving: 283 calories, 42.4g protein, 1.6g carbohydrates, 10.9g fat, 0.2g fiber, 130mg cholesterol, 514mg sodium, 377mg potassium.

Turkey With Plums

Servings:5

Cooking Time: 8 Hours

Ingredients:

* 1-pound turkey fillet, chopped
* 1 cup plums, pitted, halved
* 1 teaspoon ground cinnamon
* 1 cup of water
* 1 teaspoon ground black pepper

Directions:

1. Mix the turkey with ground cinnamon and ground black pepper.
2. Then transfer it in the Crock Pot.
3. Add water and plums.
4. Close the lid and cook the meal on Low for 8 hours.

Nutrition Info:

* Per Serving: 94 calories, 19g protein, 2.2g carbohydrates, 0.5g fat, 0.5g fiber, 47mg cholesterol, 207mg sodium, 29mg potassium.

Butter Chicken

Servings:4

Cooking Time: 4 Hours

Ingredients:

* 12 oz chicken fillet
* ½ cup butter
* 1 teaspoon garlic powder
* 1 teaspoon salt

Directions:

1. Put all ingredients in the Crock Pot.
2. Cook them on High for 4 hours.
3. Then shred the chicken and transfer in the plates.
4. Sprinkle the chicken with fragrant butter from the Crock Pot.

Nutrition Info:

* Per Serving: 367 calories, 25g protein, 0.5g carbohydrates, 29.3g fat, 0.1g fiber, 137mg cholesterol, 818mg sodium, 221mg potassium.

Wine Chicken

Servings:4
Cooking Time: 3 Hours
Ingredients:
- 1 cup red wine
- 1-pound chicken breast, skinless, boneless, chopped
- 1 anise star
- 1 teaspoon cayenne pepper
- 2 garlic cloves, crushed

Directions:
1. Pour red wine in the Crock Pot.
2. Add anise star, cayenne pepper, and garlic cloves.
3. Then add chopped chicken and close the lid.
4. Cook the meal on High for 3 hours.
5. Serve the chicken with hot wine sauce.

Nutrition Info:
- Per Serving: 182 calories, 24.2g protein, 2.4g carbohydrates, 2.9g fat, 0.2g fiber, 73mg cholesterol, 61mg sodium, 493mg potassium.

Italian Style Tenders

Servings:4
Cooking Time: 3 Hours
Ingredients:
- 12 oz chicken fillet
- 1 tablespoon Italian seasonings
- ½ cup of water
- 1 tablespoon olive oil
- 1 teaspoon salt

Directions:
1. Cut the chicken into tenders and sprinkle with salt and Italian seasonings.
2. Then heat the oil in the skillet.
3. Add chicken tenders and cook them on high heat for 1 minute per side.
4. Then put the chicken tenders in the Crock Pot.
5. Add water and close the lid.
6. Cook the chicken for 3 hours on High.

Nutrition Info:
- Per Serving: 202 calories, 24.6g protein, 0.4g carbohydrates, 10.8g fat, 0g fiber, 75mg cholesterol, 657mg sodium, 209mg potassium.

Tender Duck Fillets

Servings:3
Cooking Time: 8 Hours
Ingredients:
- 1 tablespoon butter
- 1 teaspoon dried rosemary
- 1 teaspoon ground nutmeg
- 9 oz duck fillet
- 1 cup of water

Directions:
1. Slice the fillet.
2. Then melt the butter in the skillet.
3. Add sliced duck fillet and roast it for 2-3 minutes per side on medium heat.
4. Transfer the roasted duck fillet and butter in the Crock Pot.
5. Add dried rosemary, ground nutmeg, and water.
6. Close the lid and cook the meal on Low for 8 hours.

Nutrition Info:
- Per Serving: 145 calories, 25.2g protein, 0.6g carbohydrates, 4.7g fat, 0.3g fiber, 10mg cholesterol, 158mg sodium, 61mg potassium.

Chicken And Green Onion Sauce

Servings: 4
Cooking Time: 4 Hours
Ingredients:
- 2 tablespoons butter, melted
- 4 green onions, chopped
- 4 chicken breast halves, skinless and boneless
- Salt and black pepper to the taste
- 8 ounces sour cream

Directions:
1. In your Crock Pot, mix chicken with melted butter, green onion, salt, pepper and sour cream, cover and cook on High for 4 hours.
2. Divide chicken between plates, drizzle green onions sauce all over and serve.

Nutrition Info:
- calories 200, fat 7, fiber 2, carbs 11, protein 20

Creamy Chicken

Servings: 4
Cooking Time: 4 Hrs
Ingredients:
- 4 chicken thighs
- Salt and black pepper to the taste
- 1 tsp onion powder
- ¼ cup sour cream
- 2 tbsp sweet paprika

Directions:
1. Add chicken, paprika, salt, black pepper, onion powder, and sour cream to the Crock Pot.

2. Put the cooker's lid on and set the cooking time to 4 hours on High settings.

3. Serve warm.

Nutrition Info:

• Per Serving: Calories: 384, Total Fat: 31g, Fiber: 2g, Total Carbs: 11g, Protein: 33g

Chicken Piccata

Servings:4

Cooking Time: 8 Hours

Ingredients:

• 4 chicken breasts, skin and bones removed

• Salt and pepper to taste

• ¼ cup butter, cubed

• ¼ cup chicken broth

• 1 tablespoon lemon juice

Directions:

1. Place all ingredients in the crockpot.

2. Give a good stir to combine everything.

3. Close the lid and cook on low for 8 hours or on high for 6 hours.

Nutrition Info:

• Calories per serving: 265; Carbohydrates:2.3 g; Protein:24 g; Fat: 14g; Sugar: 0g; Sodium:442 mg; Fiber:0 g

Chicken In Sweet Soy Sauce

Servings:6

Cooking Time: 6 Hours

Ingredients:

• ½ cup of soy sauce

• 2 teaspoons maple syrup

• ½ teaspoon ground cinnamon

• 6 chicken thighs, skinless, boneless

• ¼ cup of water

Directions:

1. Pour water and soy sauce in the Crock Pot.

2. Add chicken thighs, ground cinnamon, and maple syrup.

3. Close the lid and cook the meal on Low for 6 hours.

Nutrition Info:

• Per Serving: 295 calories, 43.6g protein, 3.3g carbohydrates, 10.8g fat, 0.3g fiber, 130mg cholesterol, 1324mg sodium, 406mg potassium.

Lemon Parsley Chicken

Servings:4

Cooking Time: 8 Hours

Ingredients:

• 2 tablespoons butter, melted

• 1-pound chicken breasts, bones removed

• Salt and pepper to taste

• 1 lemon, sliced thinly

• ½ cup parsley, chopped

Directions:

1. Line the bottom of the crockpot with foil.

2. Grease the foil with melted butter.

3. Season the chicken breasts with salt and pepper to taste.

4. Arrange on the foil and place lemon slices on top.

5. Sprinkle with chopped parsley.

6. Cook on low for 8 hours or on high for 6 hours

Nutrition Info:

• Calories per serving: 303; Carbohydrates: 3.1g; Protein: 34.5g; Fat: 14g; Sugar: 0.7g; Sodium: 430mg; Fiber: 1g

Salsa Chicken Wings

Servings:5

Cooking Time: 6 Hours

Ingredients:

• 2-pounds chicken wings

• 2 cups salsa

• ½ cup of water

Directions:

1. Put all ingredients in the Crock Pot.

2. Carefully mix the mixture and close the lid.

3. Cook the chicken wings on low for 6 hours.

Nutrition Info:

• Per Serving: 373 calories, 54.1g protein, 6.5g carbohydrates, 13.6g fat, 1.7g fiber, 161mg cholesterol, 781mg sodium, 750mg potassium.

Garlic Duck

Servings:4

Cooking Time: 5 Hours

Ingredients:

• 1-pound duck fillet

• 1 tablespoon minced garlic

• 1 tablespoon butter, softened

• 1 teaspoon dried thyme

• 1/3 cup coconut cream

Directions:

1. Mix minced garlic with butter, and dried thyme.

2. Then rub the suck fillet with garlic mixture and place it in the Crock Pot.

3. Add coconut cream and cook the duck on High for 5 hours.

4. Then slice the cooked duck fillet and sprinkle it with hot garlic coconut milk.

Nutrition Info:

- Per Serving: 216 calories, 34.1g protein, 2g carbohydrates, 8.4g fat, 0.6g fiber, 8mg cholesterol, 194mg sodium, 135mg potassium.

Chicken Masala

Servings:4
Cooking Time: 4 Hours

Ingredients:

- 1 teaspoon garam masala
- 1 teaspoon ground ginger
- 1 cup of coconut milk
- 1-pound chicken fillet, sliced
- 1 teaspoon olive oil

Directions:

1. Mix coconut milk with ground ginger, garam masala, and olive oil.
2. Add chicken fillet and mix the ingredients.
3. Then transfer them in the Crock Pot and cook on High for 4 hours.

Nutrition Info:

- Per Serving: 365 calories, 34.2g protein, 3.6g carbohydrates, 23.9g fat, 1.4g fiber, 101mg cholesterol, 108mg sodium, 439mg potassium.

Chicken Pate

Servings:6
Cooking Time: 8 Hours

Ingredients:

- 1 carrot, peeled
- 1 teaspoon salt
- 1-pound chicken liver
- 2 cups of water
- 2 tablespoons coconut oil

Directions:

1. Chop the carrot roughly and put it in the Crock Pot.
2. Add chicken liver and water.
3. Cook the mixture for 8 hours on Low.
4. Then drain water and transfer the mixture in the blender.
5. Add coconut oil and salt.
6. Blend the mixture until smooth.
7. Store the pate in the fridge for up to 7 days.

Nutrition Info:

- Per Serving: 169 calories, 18.6g protein, 1.7g carbohydrates, 9.5g fat, 0.3g fiber, 426mg cholesterol, 454mg sodium, 232mg potassium.

Stuffed Whole Chicken

Servings:10
Cooking Time: 6 Hours

Ingredients:

- 3-pound whole chicken
- 1 tablespoon taco seasonings
- 1 cup apples, chopped
- 1 tablespoon olive oil
- 2 cups of water

Directions:

1. Fill the chicken with apples.
2. Then rub the chicken with taco seasonings and brush with olive oil.
3. Place it in the Crock Pot. Add water.
4. Cook the chicken on High for 6 hours.
5. When the chicken is cooked, chop it into servings and serve with cooked apples.

Nutrition Info:

- Per Serving: 285 calories, 39.4g protein, 3.7g carbohydrates, 11.5g fat, 0.5g fiber, 121mg cholesterol, 182mg sodium, 355mg potassium.

Horseradish Chicken Wings

Servings:4
Cooking Time: 6 Hours

Ingredients:

- 3 tablespoons horseradish, grated
- 1 teaspoon ketchup
- 1 tablespoon mayonnaise
- ½ cup of water
- 1-pound chicken wings

Directions:

1. Mix chicken wings with ketchup, horseradish, and mayonnaise,
2. Put them in the Crock Pot and add water.
3. Cook the meal on Low for 6 hours.

Nutrition Info:

- Per Serving: 236 calories, 33g protein, 2.5g carbohydrates, 9.7g fat, 0.4g fiber, 102mg cholesterol, 174mg sodium, 309mg potassium.

Chicken Vegetable Curry

Servings:6
Cooking Time: 8 Hours

Ingredients:
- 1 tablespoon butter
- 1-pound chicken breasts, bones removed
- 1 package frozen vegetable mix
- 1 cup water
- 2 tablespoons curry powder

Directions:
1. Place all ingredients in the crockpot.
2. Stir to combine everything.
3. Close the lid and cook on low for 8 hours or on high for 6 hours.

Nutrition Info:
- Calories per serving: 273; Carbohydrates: 6.1g; Protein:21 g; Fat: 10g; Sugar: 0.1g; Sodium: 311mg; Fiber: 4g

Chicken Parm

Servings:3
Cooking Time: 4 Hours

Ingredients:
- 9 oz chicken fillet
- 1/3 cup cream
- 3 oz Parmesan, grated
- 1 teaspoon olive oil

Directions:
1. Brush the Crock Pot bowl with olive oil from inside.
2. Then slice the chicken fillet and place it in the Crock Pot.
3. Top it with Parmesan and cream.
4. Close the lid and cook the meal on High for 4 hours.

Nutrition Info:
- Per Serving: 283 calories, 33.9g protein, 1.8g carbohydrates, 15.4g fat, 0g fiber, 101mg cholesterol, 345mg sodium, 216mg potassium.

Spicy Almond-crusted Chicken Nuggets In The Crockpot

Servings:6
Cooking Time: 8 Hours

Ingredients:
- ¼ cup butter, melted
- 1 ½ cups almond meal
- 1 ½ cups grated parmesan cheese
- 1 ½ pounds boneless chicken breasts, cut into strips
- 2 eggs, beaten

Directions:
1. Place foil at the bottom of the crockpot.
2. Combine the almond meal and parmesan cheese.
3. Dip the chicken strips into the eggs and dredge into the parmesan and cheese mixture.
4. Place carefully in the crockpot.
5. Close the lid and cook on low for 8 hours or on high for 6 hours.

Nutrition Info:
- Calories per serving: 371; Carbohydrates: 2.5g; Protein:29 g; Fat: 22g; Sugar: 0.8g; Sodium: 527mg; Fiber: 1.4g

Almond-stuffed Chicken

Servings:6
Cooking Time: 8 Hours

Ingredients:
- 1 ½ teaspoons butter
- 1/3 cup Boursin cheese or any herbed cheese of your choice
- ¼ cup slivered almonds, toasted and chopped
- 4 boneless chicken breasts, halved
- Salt and pepper to taste

Directions:
1. Line the bottom of the crockpot with foil.
2. Grease the foil with butter.
3. In a mixing bowl, mix together the cheese and almonds.
4. Cut a slit through the chicken breasts to create a pocket.
5. Season the chicken with salt and pepper to taste.
6. Spoon the cheese mixture into the slit on the chicken. Secure the slit with toothpicks.
7. Place the chicken in the foil-lined crockpot.
8. Cover with lid and cook on low for 8 hours or on high for 6 hours.

Nutrition Info:
- Calories per serving: 249; Carbohydrates: 0.9g; Protein: 42.1g; Fat: 10g; Sugar: 0g; Sodium:592 mg; Fiber:0.4 g

Buffalo Chicken Tenders

Servings:4
Cooking Time: 3.5 Hours

Ingredients:
- 12 oz chicken fillet
- 3 tablespoons buffalo sauce
- ½ cup of coconut milk

- 1 jalapeno pepper, chopped

Directions:

1. Cut the chicken fillet into tenders and sprinkle the buffalo sauce.

2. Put the chicken tenders in the Crock Pot.

3. Add coconut milk and jalapeno pepper.

4. Close the lid and cook the meal on high for 3.5 hours.

Nutrition Info:

- Per Serving: 235 calories, 25.3g protein, 2.4g carbohydrates, 13.5g fat, 1g fiber, 76mg cholesterol, 318mg sodium, 293mg potassium.

Lemony Chicken

Servings: 6

Cooking Time: 4 Hours

Ingredients:

- 1 whole chicken, cut into medium pieces
- Salt and black pepper to the taste
- Zest of 2 lemons
- Juice of 2 lemons
- Lemon rinds from 2 lemons

Directions:

1. Put chicken pieces in your Crock Pot, season with salt and pepper to the taste, drizzle lemon juice, add lemon zest and lemon rinds, cover and cook on High for 4 hours.

2. Discard lemon rinds, divide chicken between plates, drizzle sauce from the Crock Pot over it and serve.

Nutrition Info:

- calories 334, fat 24, fiber 2, carbs 4.5, protein 27

Fanta Chicken

Servings:4

Cooking Time: 4.5 Hours

Ingredients:

- 1 cup Fanta
- 1-pound chicken breast, skinless, boneless, chopped
- 1 teaspoon ground cumin
- 1 teaspoon ground nutmeg

Directions:

1. Mix chicken breast with cumin and ground nutmeg and transfer in the Crock Pot.

2. Add Fanta and close the lid.

3. Cook the meal on high for 4.5 hours.

Nutrition Info:

- Per Serving: 162 calories, 24.2g protein, 9.3g carbohydrates, 3.2g fat, 0.2g fiber, 73mg cholesterol, 68mg sodium, 431mg potassium.

Asian Sesame Chicken

Servings:12

Cooking Time: 8 Hours

Ingredients:

- 12 chicken thighs, bones and skin removed
- 2 tablespoons sesame oil
- 3 tablespoons water
- 3 tablespoons soy sauce
- 1 thumb-size ginger, sliced thinly

Directions:

1. Place all ingredients in the crockpot.

2. Stir all ingredients to combine.

3. Close the lid and cook on low for 8 hours or on high for 6 hours.

4. Once cooked, garnish with toasted sesame seeds.

Nutrition Info:

- Calories per serving: 458; Carbohydrates: 1.5g; Protein: 32.2g; Fat: 35.05g; Sugar: 0g; Sodium: 426mg; Fiber: 0.4g

Chicken With Basil And Tomatoes

Servings:4

Cooking Time: 8 Hours

Ingredients:

- ¾ cup balsamic vinegar
- ¼ cup fresh basil leaves
- 2 tablespoons olive oil
- 8 plum tomatoes, sliced
- 4 boneless chicken breasts, bone and skin removed

Directions:

1. Place balsamic vinegar, basil leaves, olive oil and tomatoes in a blender. Season with salt and pepper to taste. Pulse until fine.

2. Arrange the chicken pieces in the crockpot.

3. Pour over the sauce.

4. Close the lid and cook on low for 8 hours or on high for 6 hours.

Nutrition Info:

- Calories per serving: 177; Carbohydrates:4 g; Protein:24 g; Fat: 115g; Sugar: 0g; Sodium: 171mg; Fiber: 3.5g

Chicken Wings In Vodka Sauce

Servings:4
Cooking Time: 6 Hours
Ingredients:
- 1-pound chicken wings
- ½ cup vodka sauce
- 1 tablespoon olive oil

Directions:
1. Put all ingredients in the Crock Pot and mix well.
2. Close the lid and cook the meal on Low for 6 hours.

Nutrition Info:
- Per Serving: 273 calories, 34.1g protein, 2.8g carbohydrates, 13.2g fat, 0g fiber, 102mg cholesterol, 208mg sodium, 276mg potassium.

Bacon Chicken Wings

Servings:4
Cooking Time: 3 Hours
Ingredients:
- 4 chicken wings, boneless
- 4 bacon slices
- 1 tablespoon maple syrup
- ½ teaspoon ground black pepper
- ½ cup of water

Directions:
1. Sprinkle the chicken wings with ground black pepper and maple syrup.
2. Then wrap every chicken wing in the bacon and place it in the Crock Pot.
3. Add water and close the lid.
4. Cook the chicken wings in High for 3 hours.

Nutrition Info:
- Per Serving: 367 calories, 16.1g protein, 25.8g carbohydrates, 22g fat, 1.1g fiber, 41mg cholesterol, 840mg sodium, 121mg potassium.

Harissa Chicken Breasts

Servings:6
Cooking Time: 8 Hours
Ingredients:
- 1 tablespoon olive oil
- 1-pound chicken breasts, skin and bones removed
- Salt to taste
- 2 tablespoon Harissa or Sriracha sauce
- 2 tablespoons toasted sesame seeds

Directions:
1. Pour oil in the crockpot.
2. Arrange the chicken breasts and season with salt and pepper to taste

3. Stir in the Sriracha or Harissa sauce. Give a good stir to incorporate everything.
4. Close the lid and cook on low for 8 hours or on high for 6 hours.
5. Once cooked, sprinkle toasted sesame seeds on top.

Nutrition Info:
- Calories per serving: 167; Carbohydrates: 1.1g; Protein: 16.3g; Fat: 10.6g; Sugar: 0g; Sodium: 632mg; Fiber: 0.6g

Halved Chicken

Servings:4
Cooking Time: 5 Hours
Ingredients:
- 2-pounds whole chicken, halved
- 1 tablespoon salt
- 1 teaspoon ground black pepper
- 2 tablespoons mayonnaise
- ½ cup of water

Directions:
1. Mix the ground black pepper with salt and mayonnaise.
2. Then rub the chicken halves with mayonnaise mixture and transfer in the Crock Pot.
3. Add water and close the lid.
4. Cook the chicken on High for 5 hours.

Nutrition Info:
- Per Serving: 461 calories, 65.7g protein, 2.1g carbohydrates, 19.3g fat, 1.2g fiber, 0.1mg cholesterol, 1993mg sodium, 559mg potassium.

Mexican Chicken In Crockpot

Servings:4
Cooking Time: 8 Hours
Ingredients:
- 2 tablespoons butter
- 1 can diced tomatoes, undrained
- 2 cups chicken, cubed
- Salt and pepper to taste
- 1 teaspoon cumin

Directions:
1. Place all ingredients in the crockpot.
2. Mix everything to combine.
3. Close the lid and cook on low for 8 hours or on high for 5 hours.

Nutrition Info:
- Calories per serving: 594; Carbohydrates: 2.9g; Protein: 97.3 g; Fat: 21.7g; Sugar: 0.5g; Sodium: 637mg; Fiber: 0.8g

Chicken With Figs

Servings:4
Cooking Time: 7 Hours
Ingredients:
- 5 oz fresh figs, chopped
- 14 oz chicken fillet, chopped
- 1 cup of water
- 1 teaspoon peppercorns
- 1 tablespoon dried dill

Directions:
1. Put all ingredients in the Crock Pot.
2. Close the lid and cook the meal on Low for 7 hours.

Nutrition Info:
- Per Serving: 280 calories, 30.1g protein, 23.4g carbohydrates, 7.7g fat, 3.7g fiber, 88mg cholesterol, 93mg sodium, 515mg potassium.

Vinegar Chicken Wings

Servings:8
Cooking Time: 3 Hours
Ingredients:
- ½ cup apple cider vinegar
- 1 teaspoon garlic powder
- 1 teaspoon smoked paprika
- ½ cup plain yogurt
- 3-pounds chicken wings

Directions:
1. Mix plain yogurt with smoked paprika, garlic powder, and apple cider vinegar.
2. Pour the liquid in the Crock Pot.
3. Add chicken wings and close the lid.
4. Cook the meal on High for 3 hours.

Nutrition Info:
- Per Serving: 339 calories, 50.2g protein, 1.6g carbohydrates, 12.8g fat, 0.1g fiber, 152mg cholesterol, 158mg sodium, 470mg potassium.

Chicken Sausages In Jam

Servings:4
Cooking Time: 6 Hours
Ingredients:
- ½ cup of strawberry jam
- ½ cup of water
- 1-pound chicken breast, skinless, boneless, chopped
- 1 teaspoon white pepper

Directions:
1. Sprinkle the chicken meat with white pepper and put it in the Crock Pot.

2. Then mix jam with water and pour the liquid over the chicken.
3. Close the lid and cook it on Low for 6 hours.

Nutrition Info:
- Per Serving: 282 calories, 24.1g protein, 37.5g carbohydrates, 2.9g fat, 0.1g fiber, 73mg cholesterol, 59mg sodium, 427mg potassium.

Garlic Pulled Chicken

Servings:4
Cooking Time: 4 Hours
Ingredients:
- 1-pound chicken breast, skinless, boneless
- 1 tablespoon minced garlic
- 2 cups of water
- ½ cup plain yogurt

Directions:
1. Put the chicken breast in the Crock Pot.
2. Add minced garlic and water.
3. Close the lid and cook the chicken on High for 4 hours.
4. Then drain water and shred the chicken breast.
5. Add plain yogurt and stir the pulled chicken well.

Nutrition Info:
- Per Serving: 154 calories, 25.9g protein, 2.9g carbohydrates, 3.2g fat, 0g fiber, 74mg cholesterol, 83mg sodium, 501mg potassium.

Lemon Garlic Dump Chicken

Servings:6
Cooking Time: 8 Hours
Ingredients:
- ¼ cup olive oil
- 2 teaspoon garlic, minced
- 6 chicken breasts, bones removed
- 1 tablespoon parsley, chopped
- 2 tablespoons lemon juice, freshly squeezed

Directions:
1. Heat oil in a skillet over medium flame.
2. Sauté the garlic until golden brown.
3. Arrange the chicken breasts in the crockpot.
4. Pour over the oil with garlic.
5. Add the parsley and lemon juice. Add a little water.
6. Close the lid and cook on low for 8 hours or on high for 6 hours.

Nutrition Info:
- Calories per serving: 581; Carbohydrates: 0.7g; Protein: 60.5g; Fat: 35.8g; Sugar: 0g; Sodium: 583mg; Fiber: 0.3g

Thyme Whole Chicken

Servings:6
Cooking Time: 9 Hours

Ingredients:

- 1.5-pound whole chicken
- 1 tablespoon dried thyme
- 1 tablespoon olive oil
- 1 teaspoon salt
- 1 cup of water

Directions:

1. Chop the whole chicken roughly and sprinkle with dried thyme, olive oil, and salt.
2. Then transfer it in the Crock Pot, add water.
3. Cook the chicken on low for 9 hours.

Nutrition Info:

- Per Serving: 237 calories, 32.9g protein, 0.3g carbohydrates, 10.8g fat, 0.2g fiber, 101mg cholesterol, 487mg sodium, 280mg potassium.

Basic Shredded Chicken

Servings:12
Cooking Time: 8 Hours

Ingredients:

- 6 pounds chicken breasts, bones and skin removed
- 1 teaspoon salt
- ½ teaspoon black pepper
- 5 cups homemade chicken broth
- 4 tablespoons butter

Directions:

1. Place all ingredients in the CrockPot.
2. Close the lid and cook on high for 6 hours or on low for 8 hours.
3. Shred the chicken meat using two forks.
4. Return to the CrockPot and cook on high for another 30 minutes.

Nutrition Info:

- Calories per serving: 421; Carbohydrates: 0.5g; Protein: 48.1g; Fat: 25.4g; Sugar: 0g; Sodium: 802mg; Fiber: 0.1g

Stuffed Chicken Fillets

Servings:6
Cooking Time: 4 Hours

Ingredients:

- ½ cup green peas, cooked
- ½ cup long-grain rice, cooked
- 16 oz chicken fillets
- 1 cup of water
- 1 teaspoon Italian seasonings

Directions:

1. Make the horizontal cuts in chicken fillets.
2. After this, mix Italian seasonings with rice and green peas.
3. Fill the chicken fillet with rice mixture and secure them with toothpicks.
4. Put the chicken fillets in the Crock Pot.
5. Add water and close the lid.
6. Cook the chicken on high for 4 hours.

Nutrition Info:

- Per Serving: 212 calories, 23.6g protein, 14.2g carbohydrates, 6g fat, 0.8g fiber, 68mg cholesterol, 68mg sodium, 232mg potassium.

Chili Sausages

Servings:4
Cooking Time: 3 Hours

Ingredients:

- 1-pound chicken sausages, roughly chopped
- ½ cup of water
- 1 tablespoon chili powder
- 1 teaspoon tomato paste

Directions:

1. Sprinkle the chicken sausages with chili powder and transfer in the Crock Pot.
2. Then mix water and tomato paste and pour the liquid over the chicken sausages.
3. Close the lid and cook the meal on High for 3 hours.

Nutrition Info:

- Per Serving: 221 calories, 15g protein, 8.9g carbohydrates, 12.8g fat, 1.4g fiber, 0mg cholesterol, 475mg sodium, 50mg potassium.

Rosemary Rotisserie Chicken

Servings:12
Cooking Time: 12 Hours

Ingredients:

- 1-gallon water
- ¾ cup salt
- ½ cup butter
- 2 tablespoons rosemary and other herbs of your choice
- 1 whole chicken, excess fat removed

Directions:

1. In a pot, combine the water, salt, sugar, and herbs.
2. Stir to dissolve the salt and sugar.
3. Submerge the chicken completely and allow to sit in the brine for 12 hours inside the fridge.

4. Line the crockpot with tin foil.

5. Place the chicken and cook on low for 12 hours or on high for 7 hours.

Nutrition Info:

- Calories per serving: 194; Carbohydrates: 1.4g; Protein:20.6 g; Fat:6.2g; Sugar: 0g; Sodium: 562mg; Fiber: 0.9g

Chicken With Green Onion Sauce

Servings: 4
Cooking Time: 4 Hrs
Ingredients:

- 2 tbsp butter, melted
- 4 green onions, chopped
- 4 chicken breast halves, skinless and boneless
- Salt and black pepper to the taste
- 8 oz. sour cream

Directions:

1. Add melted butter, chicken, and all other ingredients to the Crock Pot.

2. Put the cooker's lid on and set the cooking time to 4 hours on High settings.

3. Serve warm.

Nutrition Info:

- Per Serving: Calories: 200, Total Fat: 7g, Fiber: 2g, Total Carbs: 11g, Protein: 20g

Chicken With Peach And Orange Sauce

Servings: 8
Cooking Time: 6 Hours
Ingredients:

- 6 chicken breasts, skinless and boneless
- 12 ounces orange juice
- 2 tablespoons lemon juice
- 15 ounces canned peaches and their juice
- 1 teaspoon soy sauce

Directions:

1. In your Crock Pot, mix chicken with orange juice, lemon juice, peaches and soy sauce, toss, cover and cook on Low for 6 hours.

2. Divide chicken breasts on plates, drizzle peach and orange sauce all over and serve.

Nutrition Info:

- calories 251, fat 4, fiber 6, carbs 18, protein 14

Continental Beef Chicken

Servings:5
Cooking Time: 9 Hours

Ingredients:

- 6 oz. dried beef
- 12 oz. chicken breast, diced
- 7 oz. sour cream
- 1 can onion soup
- 3 tbsp flour

Directions:

1. Spread half of the dried beef in the Crock Pot.

2. Top it with chicken breast, sour cream, onion soup, and flour.

3. Spread the remaining dried beef on top.

4. Put the cooker's lid on and set the cooking time to 9 hours on Low settings.

5. Serve warm.

Nutrition Info:

- Per Serving: Calories: 285, Total Fat: 15.1g, Fiber: 1g, Total Carbs: 12.56g, Protein: 24g

Chicken And Sour Cream

Servings: 4
Cooking Time: 4 Hours
Ingredients:

- 4 chicken thighs
- Salt and black pepper to the taste
- 1 teaspoon onion powder
- ¼ cup sour cream
- 2 tablespoons sweet paprika

Directions:

1. In a bowl, mix paprika with salt, pepper and onion powder and stir.

2. Season chicken pieces with this paprika mix, place them in your Crock Pot, add sour cream, toss, cover and cook on High for 4 hours.

3. Divide everything between plates and serve.

Nutrition Info:

- calories 384, fat 31, fiber 2, carbs 11, protein 33

Cilantro Lime Chicken

Servings:3
Cooking Time: 8 Hours
Ingredients:

- 3 chicken breasts, bones and skin removed
- Juice from 3 limes, freshly squeezed
- 6 cloves of garlic, minced
- 1 teaspoon cumin
- ¼ cup cilantro

Directions:

1. Place all ingredients in the crockpot.

2. Give a stir to mix everything.

3. Close the lid and cook on low for 8 hours or on high for 6 hours.

Nutrition Info:

• Calories per serving: 522; Carbohydrates: 6.1g; Protein: 61.8g; Fat: 27.1g; Sugar: 2.3g; Sodium: 453mg; Fiber: 1.2g

Jalapeno Chicken Wings

Servings:6

Cooking Time: 3 Hours

Ingredients:

• 5 jalapenos, minced
• ½ cup tomato juice
• 2-pounds chicken wings, skinless
• 1 teaspoon salt
• ¼ cup of water

Directions:

1. Mix minced jalapenos with tomato juice, salt, and water.
2. Pour the liquid in the Crock Pot.
3. Add chicken wings and close the lid.
4. Cook the meal on High for 3 hours.

Nutrition Info:

• Per Serving: 294 calories, 44.1g protein, 1.6g carbohydrates, 11.3g fat, 0.4g fiber, 135mg cholesterol, 573mg sodium, 439mg potassium.

Greece Style Chicken

Servings:6

Cooking Time: 8 Hours

Ingredients:

• 12 oz chicken fillet, chopped
• 1 cup green olives, chopped
• 1 cup of water
• 1 tablespoon cream cheese

• ½ teaspoon dried thyme

Directions:

1. Put all ingredients in the Crock Pot.
2. Close the lid and cook the meal on Low for 8 hours.
3. Then transfer the cooked chicken in the bowls and top with olives and hot liquid from the Crock Pot.

Nutrition Info:

• Per Serving: 124 calories,16.7g protein, 0.8g carbohydrates, 5.7g fat, 0.3g fiber, 52mg cholesterol, 167mg sodium, 142mg potassium.

Chicken, Peppers And Onions

Servings:4

Cooking Time: 8 Hours

Ingredients:

• 1 tablespoon olive oil
• ½ cup shallots, peeled
• 1-pound boneless chicken breasts, sliced
• ½ cup green and red peppers, diced
• Salt and pepper to taste

Directions:

1. Heat oil in a skillet over medium flame.
2. Sauté the shallots until fragrant and translucent. Allow to cook so that the outer edges of the shallots turn slightly brown.
3. Transfer into the crockpot.
4. Add the chicken breasts and the peppers.
5. Season with salt and pepper to taste.
6. Add a few tablespoons of water.
7. Close the lid and cook on low for 8 hours or on high for 6 hours.

Nutrition Info:

• Calories per serving: 179; Carbohydrates: 3.05g; Protein:26.1 g; Fat: 10.4g; Sugar: 0g; Sodium: 538mg; Fiber:2.4 g

Fish & Seafood Recipes

Turmeric Mackerel

Servings:4

Cooking Time: 2.5 Hours

Ingredients:

• 1-pound mackerel fillet
• 1 tablespoon ground turmeric
• ½ teaspoon salt
• ¼ teaspoon chili powder
• ½ cup of water

Directions:

1. Rub the mackerel fillet with ground turmeric and chili powder.
2. Then put it in the Crock Pot.
3. Add water and salt.
4. Close the lid and cook the fish on High for 2.5 hours.

Nutrition Info:

• Per Serving: 304 calories, 27.2g protein, 1.2g carbohydrates, 20.4g fat, 0.4g fiber, 58mg cholesterol, 388mg sodium, 501mg potassium

Paprika Shrimp

Servings: 3
Cooking Time: 4 Hours 20 Minutes
Ingredients:
- 1 pound tiger shrimp
- Salt, to taste
- ½ teaspoon smoked paprika
- 2 tablespoons tea seed oil

Directions:
1. Mix together all the ingredients in a large bowl until well combined.
2. Transfer the shrimp in the crock pot and cover the lid.
3. Cook on LOW for about 4 hours and dish out to serve with roasted tomatoes and jalapenos.

Nutrition Info:
- Calories: 231 Fat: 10.4g Carbohydrates: 0.2g

Butter Crab Legs

Servings:4
Cooking Time: 45 Minutes
Ingredients:
- 15 oz king crab legs
- 1 tablespoon butter
- 1 cup of water
- 1 teaspoon dried basil

Directions:
1. Put the crab legs in the Crock Pot.
2. Add basil and water and cook them on High for 45 minutes.

Nutrition Info:
- Per Serving: 133 calories, 20.4g protein, 0g carbohydrates, 4.5g fat, 0g fiber, 67mg cholesterol, 1161mg sodium, 2mg potassium

Easy Salmon And Kimchi Sauce

Servings: 4
Cooking Time: 2 Hours
Ingredients:
- 2 tablespoons butter, soft
- 1 and ¼ pound salmon fillet
- 2 ounces Kimchi, finely chopped
- Salt and black pepper to the taste

Directions:
1. In your food processor, mix butter with Kimchi, blend well, rub salmon with salt, pepper and Kimchi mix, place in your Crock Pot, cover and cook on High for 2 hours.
2. Divide between plates and serve with a side salad.

Nutrition Info:
- calories 270, fat 12, fiber 5, carbs 13, protein 21

Vegan Milk Clams

Servings:4
Cooking Time: 3 Hours
Ingredients:
- 1 cup organic almond milk
- 1 teaspoon dried parsley
- 1 teaspoon dried dill
- ½ teaspoon salt
- 1-pound clams

Directions:
1. Put all ingredients in the Crock Pot and gently mix.
2. Close the lid and cook the clams on Low for 3 hours.

Nutrition Info:
- Per Serving: 70 calories, 1g protein, 14.6g carbohydrates, 0.9g fat, 0.5g fiber, 0mg cholesterol, 737mg sodium, 111mg potassium

Scallops With Sour Cream And Dill

Servings:4
Cooking Time: 2 Hours
Ingredients:
- 1 ¼ pounds scallops
- Salt and pepper to taste
- 3 teaspoons butter
- ¼ cup sour cream
- 1 tablespoon fresh dill

Directions:
1. Add all ingredients into the crockpot.
2. Give a good stir to combine everything.
3. Close the lid and cook on high for 30 minutes or on low for 2 hours.

Nutrition Info:
- Calories per serving: 152; Carbohydrates: 4.3g; Protein: 18.2g; Fat: 5.7g; Sugar: 0.5g; Sodium: 231mg; Fiber: 2.3g

Soy Sauce Scallops

Servings:4
Cooking Time: 30 Minutes
Ingredients:
- ¼ cup of soy sauce
- 1 tablespoon butter
- ½ teaspoon white pepper
- 1-pound scallops

Directions:
1. Pour soy sauce in the Crock Pot.

2. Add butter and white pepper.
3. After this, add scallops and close the lid.
4. Cook them on High for 30 minutes.

Nutrition Info:

- Per Serving: 134 calories, 20.1g protein, 4.1g carbohydrates, 3.8g fat, 0.2g fiber, 45mg cholesterol, 1102mg sodium, 404mg potassium

Garlic Tuna

Servings:4
Cooking Time: 2 Hours

Ingredients:

- 1-pound tuna fillet
- 1 teaspoon garlic powder
- 1 tablespoon olive oil
- ½ cup of water

Directions:

1. Sprinkle the tuna fillet with garlic powder.
2. Then pour olive oil in the skillet and heat it well.
3. Add the tuna and roast it for 1 minute per side.
4. Transfer the tuna in the Crock Pot.
5. Add water and cook it on High for 2 hours.

Nutrition Info:

- Per Serving: 444 calories, 23.9g protein, 0.5g carbohydrates, 38.7g fat, 0.1g fiber, 0mg cholesterol, 1mg sodium, 8mg potassium

Chili-rubbed Tilapia

Servings:4
Cooking Time: 4 Hours

Ingredients:

- 2 tablespoons chili powder
- ½ teaspoon garlic powder
- 1-pound tilapia
- 2 tablespoons lemon juice
- 2 tablespoons olive oil

Directions:

1. Place all ingredients in a mixing bowl. Stir to combine everything.
2. Allow to marinate in the fridge for at least 30 minutes.
3. Get a foil and place the fish including the marinade in the middle of the foil.
4. Fold the foil and crimp the edges to seal.
5. Place inside the crockpot.
6. Cook on high for 2 hours or on low for 4 hours.

Nutrition Info:

- Calories per serving: 183; Carbohydrates: 2.9g; Protein: 23.4g; Fat: 11.3g; Sugar: 0.3g; Sodium: 215mg; Fiber:1.4 g

Cod In Lemon Sauce

Servings:4
Cooking Time: 2.5 Hours

Ingredients:

- 4 cod fillets
- 4 tablespoons lemon juice
- 2 tablespoons olive oil
- ½ teaspoon fennel seeds
- ¼ cup of water

Directions:

1. Put the cod fillets in the Crock Pot.
2. Add water, fennel seeds, and olive oil.
3. Cook the fish on high for 2.5 hours.
4. Then transfer the fish in the bowls and sprinkle with lemon juice.

Nutrition Info:

- Per Serving: 155 calories, 20.2g protein, 0.5g carbohydrates, 8.2g fat, 0.2g fiber, 55mg cholesterol, 74mg sodium, 23mg potassium

Five-spice Tilapia

Servings:4
Cooking Time: 5 Hours

Ingredients:

- 4 tilapia fillets
- 1 teaspoon Chinese five-spice powder
- 1 tablespoon sesame oil
- ¼ cup gluten-free soy sauce
- 3 scallions, thinly sliced

Directions:

1. Season the tilapia fillets with the Chinese five-spice powder.
2. Place sesame oil in the crockpot and arrange the fish on top.
3. Cook on high for 2 hours and on low for 4 hours.
4. Halfway through the cooking time, flip the fish to slightly brown the other side.
5. Once cooking time is done, add the soy sauce and scallion and continue cooking for another hour.

Nutrition Info:

- Calories per serving: 153; Carbohydrates: 0.9g; Protein: 25.8g; Fat: 5.6g; Sugar: 0g; Sodium: 424mg; Fiber: 0g

Butter Smelt

Servings:4
Cooking Time: 6 Hours
Ingredients:
- 16 oz smelt fillet
- 1/3 cup butter
- 1 teaspoon dried thyme
- 1 teaspoon salt

Directions:
1. Sprinkle the fish with dried thyme and salt and put in the Crock Pot.
2. Add butter and close the lid.
3. Cook the smelt on Low for 6 hours.

Nutrition Info:
- Per Serving: 226 calories, 17.2g protein, 0.2g carbohydrates, 17.4g fat, 0.1g fiber, 191mg cholesterol, 750mg sodium, 7mg potassium

Fish Soufflé(2)

Servings:4
Cooking Time: 7 Hours
Ingredients:
- 4 eggs, beaten
- 8 oz salmon fillet, chopped
- ¼ cup of coconut milk
- 2 oz Provolone cheese, grated

Directions:
1. Mix coconut milk with eggs and pour the liquid in the Crock Pot.
2. Add salmon and cheese.
3. Close the lid and cook soufflé for 7 hours on low.

Nutrition Info:
- Per Serving: 222 calories, 20.5g protein, 1.5g carbohydrates, 15.2g fat, 0.3g fiber, 198mg cholesterol, 212mg sodium, 336mg potassium

Mustard Cod

Servings:4
Cooking Time: 3 Hours
Ingredients:
- 4 cod fillets
- 4 teaspoons mustard
- 2 tablespoons sesame oil
- ¼ cup of water

Directions:
1. Mix mustard with sesame oil.
2. Then brush the cod fillets with mustard mixture and transfer in the Crock Pot.
3. Add water and cook the fish on low for 3 hours.

Nutrition Info:
- Per Serving: 166 calories, 20.8g protein, 1.2g carbohydrates, 8.8g fat, 0.5g fiber, 55mg cholesterol, 71mg sodium, 23mg potassium

Cinnamon Catfish

Servings:2
Cooking Time: 2.5 Hours
Ingredients:
- 2 catfish fillets
- 1 teaspoon ground cinnamon
- 1 tablespoon lemon juice
- ½ teaspoon sesame oil
- 1/3 cup water

Directions:
1. Sprinkle the fish fillets with ground cinnamon, lemon juice, and sesame oil.
2. Put the fillets in the Crock Pot in one layer.
3. Add water and close the lid.
4. Cook the meal on High for 2.5 hours.

Nutrition Info:
- Per Serving: 231 calories, 25g protein, 1.1g carbohydrates, 13.3g fat, 0.6g fiber, 75mg cholesterol, 88mg sodium, 528mg potassium.

Marinara Salmon

Servings:4
Cooking Time: 3 Hours
Ingredients:
- 1-pound salmon fillet, chopped
- ½ cup marinara sauce
- ¼ cup fresh cilantro, chopped
- ¼ cup of water

Directions:
1. Put the salmon in the Crock Pot.
2. Add marinara sauce, cilantro, and water.
3. Close the lid and cook the fish on High for 3 hours.

Nutrition Info:
- Per Serving: 177 calories, 22.6g protein, 4.3g carbohydrates, 7.9g fat, 0.8g fiber, 51mg cholesterol, 179mg sodium, 540mg potassium

Crockpot Greek Snapper

Servings:8

Cooking Time: 4 Hours

Ingredients:

- 3 tablespoons olive oil
- 12 snapper fillets
- 1 tablespoon Greek seasoning
- 24 lemon slices
- Salt and pepper to taste

Directions:

1. Line the bottom of the crockpot with foil.
2. Grease the foil with olive oil
3. Season the snapper fillets with Greek seasoning, salt, and pepper.
4. Arrange lemon slices on top.
5. Close the lid and cook on high for 2 hours and on low for 4 hours.

Nutrition Info:

- Calories per serving: 409; Carbohydrates: 4.3g; Protein:67 g; Fat: 15.3g; Sugar: 0g; Sodium: 246mg; Fiber: 1.8g

Garlic Perch

Servings:4

Cooking Time: 4 Hours

Ingredients:

- 1-pound perch
- 1 teaspoon minced garlic
- 1 tablespoon butter, softened
- 1 tablespoon fish sauce
- ½ cup of water

Directions:

1. In the shallow bowl mix minced garlic, butter, and fish sauce.
2. Rub the perch with a garlic butter mixture and arrange it in the Crock Pot.
3. Add remaining garlic butter mixture and water.
4. Cook the fish on high for 4 hours.

Nutrition Info:

- Per Serving: 161 calories, 28.5g protein, 0.4g carbohydrates, 4.2g fat, 0g fiber, 138mg cholesterol, 458mg sodium, 407mg potassium.

Shrimps Boil

Servings:2

Cooking Time: 45 Minutes

Ingredients:

- ½ cup of water
- 1 tablespoon piri piri sauce
- 1 tablespoon butter
- 7 oz shrimps, peeled

Directions:

1. Pour water in the Crock Pot.
2. Add shrimps and cook them on high for 45 minutes.
3. Then drain water and transfer shrimps in the skillet.
4. Add butter and piri piri sauce.
5. Roast the shrimps for 2-3 minutes on medium heat.

Nutrition Info:

- Per Serving: 174 calories, 22.7g protein, 1.8g carbohydrates, 7.8g fat, 0.1g fiber, 224mg cholesterol, 285mg sodium, 170mg potassium

Mackerel Bites

Servings:4

Cooking Time: 3 Hours

Ingredients:

- 1-pound mackerel fillet, chopped
- 1 tablespoon avocado oil
- ½ teaspoon ground paprika
- ½ teaspoon ground turmeric
- 1/3 cup water

Directions:

1. In the shallow bowl mix ground paprika with ground turmeric.
2. Then sprinkle the mackerel fillet with a spice mixture.
3. Heat the avocado oil in the skillet well.
4. Add fish and roast it for 1 minute per side on high heat.
5. Pour water in the Crock Pot.
6. Add fish and close the lid.
7. Cook the mackerel bites on High for 3 hours.

Nutrition Info:

- Per Serving: 304 calories, 27.2g protein, 0.5g carbohydrates, 20.7g fat, 0.3g fiber, 85mg cholesterol, 95mg sodium, 479mg potassium

Hot Sauce Shrimps

Servings:4

Cooking Time: 35 Minutes

Ingredients:

- 2 tablespoons hot sauce
- 1 tablespoon sunflower oil
- 4 tablespoons lemon juice
- ¼ cup of water
- 1-pound shrimps, peeled

Directions:

1. Mix shrimps with lemon juice, sunflower oil, and hot sauce. Leave them for 20 minutes to marinate.
2. After this, transfer the shrimps in the Crock Pot. Add water.
3. Cook the shrimps on High for 35 minutes.

Nutrition Info:

- Per Serving: 170 calories, 26g protein, 2.2g carbohydrates, 5.6g fat, 0.1g fiber, 239mg cholesterol, 470mg sodium, 222mg potassium

Thyme And Sesame Halibut

Servings:2

Cooking Time: 4 Hours

Ingredients:

- 1 tablespoon lemon juice
- 1 teaspoon thyme
- Salt and pepper to taste
- 8 ounces halibut or mahi-mahi, cut into 2 portions
- 1 tablespoons sesame seeds, toasted

Directions:

1. Line the bottom of the crockpot with a foil.
2. Mix lemon juice, thyme, salt and pepper in a shallow dish.
3. Place the fish and allow to marinate for 2 hours in the fish.
4. Sprinkle the fish with toasted sesame seeds.
5. Arrange the fish in the foil-lined crockpot.
6. Close the lid and cook on high for 2 hours or on low for 4 hours.

Nutrition Info:

- Calories per serving: 238; Carbohydrates: 3.9g; Protein: 23.1g; Fat: 14.9g; Sugar: 0.5g; Sodium:313 mg; Fiber:1.6 g

Cheesy Fish Dip

Servings:6

Cooking Time: 5 Hours

Ingredients:

- ½ cup cream

- ½ cup Mozzarella, shredded
- 8 oz tuna, canned, shredded
- 2 oz chives, chopped

Directions:

1. Put all ingredients in the Crock Pot and gently mix.
2. Then close the lid and cook the fish dip in Low for 5 hours.

Nutrition Info:

- Per Serving: 93 calories, 11.2g protein, 1.1g carbohydrates, 4.7g fat, 0.2g fiber, 17mg cholesterol, 40mg sodium, 161mg potassium.

Curry Clams

Servings:4

Cooking Time: 1.5 Hour

Ingredients:

- 1-pound clams
- 1 teaspoon curry paste
- ¼ cup of coconut milk
- 1 cup of water

Directions:

1. Mix coconut milk with curry paste and water and pour it in the Crock Pot.
2. Add clams and close the lid.
3. Cook the meal on High for 1.5 hours or until the clams are opened.

Nutrition Info:

- Per Serving: 97 calories, 1.1g protein, 13.6g carbohydrates, 4.5g fat, 0.8g fiber, 0mg cholesterol, 415mg sodium, 141mg potassium.

Salmon With Lime Butter

Servings:4

Cooking Time: 4 Hours

Ingredients:

- 1-pound salmon fillet cut into 4 portions
- 1 tablespoon butter, melted
- Salt and pepper to taste
- 2 tablespoons lime juice
- ½ teaspoon lime zest, grated

Directions:

1. Add all ingredients in the crockpot.
2. Close the lid.
3. Cook on high for 2 hours and on low for 4 hours.

Nutrition Info:

- Calories per serving: 206; Carbohydrates: 1.8g; Protein:23.7 g; Fat: 15.2g; Sugar: 0g; Sodium:235 mg; Fiber: 0.5g

Butter Dipped Crab Legs

Servings: 4

Cooking Time: 1 Hr. 30 Minutes

Ingredients:

- 4 lbs. king crab legs, broken in half
- 3 lemon wedges
- ¼ cup butter, melted
- ½ cup chicken stock

Directions:

1. Add crab legs, butter, and chicken stock to the insert of the Crock Pot.
2. Put the cooker's lid on and set the cooking time to 1.5 hours on High settings.
3. Serve warm with lemon wedges.

Nutrition Info:

- Per Serving: Calories: 100, Total Fat: 1g, Fiber: 5g, Total Carbs: 12g, Protein: 3g

Butter Salmon

Servings:2

Cooking Time: 1.5 Hours

Ingredients:

- 8 oz salmon fillet
- 3 tablespoons butter
- 1 teaspoon dried sage
- ¼ cup of water

Directions:

1. Churn butter with sage and preheat the mixture until liquid.
2. Then cut the salmon fillets into 2 servings and put in the Crock Pot.
3. Add water and melted butter mixture.
4. Close the lid and cook the salmon on High for 1.5 hours.

Nutrition Info:

- Per Serving: 304 calories, 22.2g protein, 0.2g carbohydrates, 24.3g fat, 0.1g fiber, 96mg cholesterol, 174mg sodium, 444mg potassium.

Sweet Milkfish Saute

Servings:4

Cooking Time: 3 Hours

Ingredients:

- 2 mangos, pitted, peeled, chopped
- 12 oz milkfish fillet, chopped
- ½ cup tomatoes, chopped
- ½ cup of water
- 1 teaspoon ground cardamom

Directions:

1. Mix mangos with tomatoes and ground cardamom.
2. Transfer the ingredients in the Crock Pot.
3. Then add milkfish fillet and water.
4. Cook the saute on High for 3 hours.
5. Carefully stir the saute before serving.

Nutrition Info:

- Per Serving: 268 calories, 24g protein, 26.4g carbohydrates, 8.1g fat, 3.1g fiber, 57mg cholesterol, 82mg sodium, 660mg potassium.

Butter Tilapia

Servings:4

Cooking Time: 6 Hours

Ingredients:

- 4 tilapia fillets
- ½ cup butter
- 1 teaspoon dried dill
- ½ teaspoon ground black pepper

Directions:

1. Sprinkle the tilapia fillets with dried dill and ground black pepper. Put them in the Crock Pot.
2. Add butter.
3. Cook the tilapia on Low for 6 hours.

Nutrition Info:

- Per Serving: 298 calories, 21.3g protein, 0.3g carbohydrates, 24.1g fat, 0.1g fiber, 116mg cholesterol, 204mg sodium, 18mg potassium

Miso-poached Cod

Servings:4

Cooking Time: 2.5 Hours

Ingredients:

- 1 teaspoon miso paste
- ½ cup of water
- ½ teaspoon dried lemongrass
- 4 cod fillets
- 1 teaspoon olive oil

Directions:

1. Mix miso paste with water, dried lemongrass, and olive oil.
2. Then pour the liquid in the Crock Pot.
3. Add cod fillets.
4. Cook the cod on High for 2.5 hours.

Nutrition Info:

- Per Serving: 103 calories, 20.2g protein, 0.4g carbohydrates, 2.3g fat, 0.1g fiber, 55mg cholesterol, 124mg sodium, 5mg potassium

Apricot And Halibut Saute

Servings:2
Cooking Time: 5 Hours
Ingredients:
- 6 oz halibut fillet, chopped
- ½ cup apricots, pitted, chopped
- ½ cup of water
- 1 tablespoon soy sauce
- 1 teaspoon ground cumin

Directions:
1. Put all ingredients in the Crock Pot.
2. Close the lid and cook the fish sauté on Low for 5 hours.

Nutrition Info:
- Per Serving: 407 calories, 28.7g protein, 5.3g carbohydrates, 28.7g fat, 0.9g fiber, 94mg cholesterol, 619mg sodium, 684mg potassium.

Chili Bigeye Jack (tuna)

Servings:4
Cooking Time: 3.5 Hours
Ingredients:
- 9 oz tuna fillet (bigeye jack), roughly chopped
- 1 teaspoon chili powder
- 1 teaspoon curry paste
- ½ cup of coconut milk
- 1 tablespoon sesame oil

Directions:
1. Mix curry paste and coconut milk and pour the liquid in the Crock Pot.
2. Add tuna fillet and sesame oil.
3. Then add chili powder.
4. Cook the meal on High for 3.5 hours.

Nutrition Info:
- Per Serving: 341 calories, 14.2g protein, 2.4g carbohydrates, 31.2g fat, 0.9g fiber, 0mg cholesterol, 11mg sodium, 91mg potassium

Spicy Curried Shrimps

Servings:4
Cooking Time: 2 Hours
Ingredients:
- 1 ½ pounds shrimp, shelled and deveined
- 1 tablespoon ghee or butter, melted
- 1 tablespoon curry powder
- 1 teaspoon cayenne pepper
- Salt and pepper to taste

Directions:

1. Place all ingredients in the crockpot.
2. Give a stir to incorporate everything.
3. Close the lid and allow to cook on low for 2 hours or on high for 30 minutes.

Nutrition Info:
- Calories per serving: 207; Carbohydrates:2.2 g; Protein: 35.2g; Fat: 10.5g; Sugar: 0g; Sodium: 325mg; Fiber: 1.6g

Coconut Curry Cod

Servings:2
Cooking Time: 2.5 Hours
Ingredients:
- 2 cod fillets
- ½ teaspoon curry paste
- 1/3 cup coconut milk
- 1 teaspoon sunflower oil

Directions:
1. Mix coconut milk with curry paste, add sunflower oil, and transfer the liquid in the Crock Pot.
2. Add cod fillets.
3. Cook the meal on High for 2.5 hours.

Nutrition Info:
- Per Serving: 211 calories, 21g protein, 2.6g carbohydrates, 13.6g fat, 0.9g fiber, 55mg cholesterol, 76mg sodium, 105mg potassium

Crockpot Smoked Trout

Servings:4
Cooking Time: 2 Hours
Ingredients:
- 2 tablespoons liquid smoke
- 2 tablespoons olive oil
- 4 ounces smoked trout, skin removed then flaked
- Salt and pepper to taste
- 2 tablespoons mustard

Directions:
1. Place all ingredients in the crockpot.
2. Cook on high for 1 hour or on low for 2 hours until the trout flakes have absorbed the sauce.

Nutrition Info:
- Calories per serving: 116; Carbohydrates: 1.5g; Protein: 7.2g; Fat: 9.2g; Sugar: 0g; Sodium: 347mg; Fiber: 1.3g

Maple Mustard Salmon

Servings: 1
Cooking Time: 2 Hrs.
Ingredients:

- 1 big salmon fillet
- Salt and black pepper to the taste
- 2 tbsp mustard
- 1 tbsp olive oil
- 1 tbsp maple extract

Directions:

1. Whisk maple extract with mustard in a bowl.
2. Place the salmon in the insert of Crock Pot.
3. Add salt, black pepper and mustard mixture over the salmon.
4. Put the cooker's lid on and set the cooking time to 2 hours on High settings.
5. Serve warm.

Nutrition Info:

- Per Serving: Calories: 240, Total Fat: 7g, Fiber: 1g, Total Carbs: 15g, Protein: 23g

Shrimps And Carrot Saute

Servings:4
Cooking Time: 6 Hours
Ingredients:

- 1 cup carrot, diced
- 1-pound shrimps, peeled
- 1 cup tomatoes, chopped
- ½ cup of water
- 1 teaspoon fennel seeds

Directions:

1. Put all ingredients in the Crock Pot.
2. Gently mix the mixture and close the lid.
3. Cook the saute on Low for 6 hours.

Nutrition Info:

- Per Serving: 156 calories, 26.5g protein, 6.4g carbohydrates, 2.1g fat, 1.4g fiber, 239mg cholesterol, 299mg sodium, 395mg potassium

Apple Cider Vinegar Sardines

Servings:4
Cooking Time: 4.5 Hours
Ingredients:

- 14 oz sardines
- 1 tablespoon butter
- ¼ cup apple cider vinegar
- ½ teaspoon cayenne pepper
- 4 tablespoons coconut cream

Directions:

1. Put sardines in the Crock Pot.
2. Add butter, apple cider vinegar, cayenne pepper, and coconut cream.

3. Close the lid and cook the meal on Low for 4.5 hours.

Nutrition Info:

- Per Serving: 270 calories, 24.8g protein, 1.1g carbohydrates, 17.9g fat, 0.4g fiber, 149mg cholesterol,525mg sodium, 450mg potassium

Cod Sticks In Blankets

Servings:4
Cooking Time: 4 Hours
Ingredients:

- 4 cod fillets
- 4 oz puff pastry
- 1 teaspoon mayonnaise
- 1 teaspoon ground black pepper
- 1 teaspoon olive oil

Directions:

1. Cut the cod fillets into the sticks.
2. Then sprinkle them with mayonnaise and ground black pepper.
3. Roll up the puff pastry and cut into strips.
4. Roll every cod stick in the puff pastry and brush with olive oil.
5. Put the cod sticks in the Crock Pot in one layer and cook on high for 4 hours.

Nutrition Info:

- Per Serving: 262 calories, 22.1g protein, 13.4g carbohydrates, 13.g fat, 0.6g fiber, 55mg cholesterol, 150mg sodium, 24mg potassium

Braised Lobster

Servings:4
Cooking Time: 3 Hours
Ingredients:

- 2-pound lobster, cleaned
- 1 cup of water
- 1 teaspoon Italian seasonings

Directions:

1. Put all ingredients in the Crock Pot.
2. Close the lid and cook the lobster in High for 3 hours.
3. Remove the lobster from the Crock Pot and cool it till room temperature

Nutrition Info:

- Per Serving: 206 calories, 43.1g protein, 0.1g carbohydrates, 2.2g fat, 0g fiber, 332mg cholesterol, 1104mg sodium, 524mg potassium.

Sweet And Sour Shrimps

Servings:2
Cooking Time: 50 Minutes
Ingredients:
- 8 oz shrimps, peeled
- ½ cup of water
- 2 tablespoons lemon juice
- 1 tablespoon maple syrup

Directions:
1. Pour water in the Crock Pot.
2. Add shrimps and cook them on High for 50 minutes.
3. Then drain water and ass lemon juice and maple syrup.
4. Carefully stir the shrimps and transfer them in the serving bowls.

Nutrition Info:
- Per Serving: 165 calories, 26g protein, 8.8g carbohydrates, 2.1g fat, 0.1g fiber, 239mg cholesterol, 282mg sodium, 232mg potassium.

Cilantro Haddock

Servings:2
Cooking Time: 1.5 Hour
Ingredients:
- 6 oz haddock fillet
- 1 teaspoon dried cilantro
- 1 teaspoon olive oil
- 1 teaspoon lemon juice
- ¼ cup fish stock

Directions:
1. Heat the olive oil in the skillet well.
2. Then put the haddock fillet and roast it for 1 minute per side.
3. Transfer the fillets in the Crock Pot.
4. Add fish stock, cilantro, and lemon juice.
5. Cook the fish on high for 1.5 hours.

Nutrition Info:
- Per Serving: 121 calories, 21.3g protein, 0.1g carbohydrates, 3.4g fat, 0g fiber, 63mg cholesterol, 120mg sodium, 385mg potassium

Braised Salmon

Servings:4
Cooking Time: 1 Hour
Ingredients:
- 1 cup of water
- 2-pound salmon fillet
- 1 teaspoon salt

- 1 teaspoon ground black pepper

Directions:
1. Put all ingredients in the Crock Pot and close the lid.
2. Cook the salmon on High for 1 hour.

Nutrition Info:
- Per Serving: 301 calories, 44.1g protein, 0.3g carbohydrates, 14g fat, 0.1g fiber, 100mg cholesterol, 683mg sodium, 878mg potassium.

Sweet And Mustard Tilapia

Servings:4
Cooking Time: 4.5 Hours
Ingredients:
- 16 oz tilapia fillets
- 1 teaspoon brown sugar
- 2 tablespoons mustard
- 1 tablespoon sesame oil
- ¼ cup of water

Directions:
1. Mix brown sugar with mustard and sesame oil.
2. Carefully rub the tilapia fillets with mustard mixture and transfer them in the Crock Pot.
3. Add water.
4. Cook the tilapia on Low for 5 hours.

Nutrition Info:
- Per Serving: 153 calories, 22.5g protein, 2.7g carbohydrates, 6g fat, 0.8g fiber, 55mg cholesterol, 41mg sodium, 39mg potassium

Crab Legs

Servings: 4
Cooking Time: 1 Hour And 30 Minutes
Ingredients:
- 4 pounds king crab legs, broken in half
- 3 lemon wedges
- ¼ cup butter, melted
- ½ cup chicken stock

Directions:
1. In your Crock Pot, mix stock with crab legs and butter, cover and cook on High for 1 hour and 30 minutes.
2. Divide crab legs between bowls, drizzle melted butter all over and serve with lemon wedges on the side.

Nutrition Info:
- calories 100, fat 1, fiber 5, carbs 12, protein 3

Bigeye Jack Saute

Servings:4
Cooking Time: 6 Hours
Ingredients:

- 7 oz (bigeye jack) tuna fillet, chopped
- 1 cup tomato, chopped
- 1 teaspoon ground black pepper
- 1 jalapeno pepper, chopped
- ½ cup chicken stock

Directions:

1. Put all ingredients in the Crock Pot and close the lid.
2. Cook the saute on Low for 6 hours.

Nutrition Info:

- Per Serving: 192 calories, 11g protein, 2.4g carbohydrates, 15.6g fat, 0.8g fiber, 0mg cholesterol, 98mg sodium, 123mg potassium

Creamy Pangasius

Servings:4
Cooking Time: 2.5 Hours
Ingredients:

- 4 pangasius fillets
- ½ cup cream
- 1 teaspoon cornflour
- 1 tablespoon fish sauce
- 1 teaspoon ground nutmeg

Directions:

1. Coat the fish fillets in the cornflour and sprinkle with ground nutmeg.
2. Put the fish in the Crock Pot.
3. Add cream and fish sauce.
4. Close the lid and cook the meal on High for 2.5 hours.

Nutrition Info:

- Per Serving: 106 calories, 15.5g protein, 1.8g carbohydrates, 4.9g fat, 0.2g fiber, 26mg cholesterol, 617mg sodium, 28mg potassium

Sriracha Cod

Servings:4
Cooking Time: 6 Hours
Ingredients:

- 4 cod fillets
- 2 tablespoons sriracha
- 1 tablespoon olive oil
- 1 teaspoon tomato paste
- ½ cup of water

Directions:

1. Sprinkle the cod fillets with sriracha, olive oil, and tomato paste.
2. Put the fish in the Crock Pot and add water.
3. Cook it on Low for 6 hours.

Nutrition Info:

- Per Serving: 129 calories, 20.1g protein, 1.8g carbohydrates, 4.5g fat, 0.1g fiber, 55mg cholesterol, 125mg sodium, 14mg potassium.

Almond-crusted Tilapia

Servings:4
Cooking Time: 4 Hours
Ingredients:

- 2 tablespoons olive oil
- 1 cup chopped almonds
- ¼ cup ground flaxseed
- 4 tilapia fillets
- Salt and pepper to taste

Directions:

1. Line the bottom of the crockpot with a foil.
2. Grease the foil with the olive oil.
3. In a mixing bowl, combine the almonds and flaxseed.
4. Season the tilapia with salt and pepper to taste.
5. Dredge the tilapia fillets with the almond and flaxseed mixture.
6. Place neatly in the foil-lined crockpot.
7. Close the lid and cook on high for 2 hours and on low for 4 hours.

Nutrition Info:

- Calories per serving: 233; Carbohydrates: 4.6g; Protein: 25.5g; Fat: 13.3g; Sugar: 0.4g; Sodium: 342mg; Fiber: 1.9g

Smelt In Avocado Oil

Servings:4
Cooking Time: 4 Hours
Ingredients:

- 12 oz smelt fillet
- 1 teaspoon chili powder
- ¼ teaspoon ground turmeric
- ½ teaspoon smoked paprika
- 4 tablespoons avocado oil

Directions:

1. Cut the smelt fillet into 4 servings.
2. Then sprinkle every fish fillet with chili powder, ground turmeric, and smoked paprika.
3. Put the fish in the Crock Pot.

4. Add avocado oil and close the lid.
5. Cook the fish on Low for 4 hours.

Nutrition Info:

- Per Serving: 89 calories, 13.1g protein, 1.4g carbohydrates, 3.5g fat, 1g fiber, 112mg cholesterol, 52mg sodium, 66mg potassium

Lunch & Dinner Recipes

Pesto Freekeh

Servings:4
Cooking Time: 2 Hours

Ingredients:

- 2 tablespoons pesto sauce
- 1 tablespoon sesame oil
- 1 oz raisins
- 1 cup freekeh
- 3 cups chicken stock

Directions:

1. Pour the chicken stock in the Crock Pot.
2. Add freekeh and raisins and cook the ingredients on High for 2 hours. The cooked freekeh should be tender.
3. Then transfer the freekeh mixture in the bowl.
4. Add sesame oil and pesto sauce.
5. Carefully mix the meal.

Nutrition Info:

- Per Serving: 125 calories, 3.5g protein, 13.2g carbohydrates, 7.4g fat, 1.4g fiber, 2mg cholesterol, 621mg sodium, 64mg potassium.

Buttered Broccoli

Servings: 4
Cooking Time: 1 1/2 Hours

Ingredients:

- 2 heads broccoli, cut into florets
- 1 shallot, sliced
- 2 garlic cloves, chopped
- 4 tablespoons butter
- Salt and pepper to taste

Directions:

1. Combine all the ingredients in your Crock Pot.
2. Add enough salt and pepper and cook the broccoli on high settings for 1 1/4 hours.
3. Serve the broccoli warm and fresh.

Sweet Farro

Servings:3
Cooking Time: 6 Hours

Ingredients:

- ½ cup farro
- 2 cups of water
- ½ cup heavy cream
- 2 tablespoons dried cranberries
- 2 tablespoons sugar

Directions:

1. Chop the cranberries and put in the Crock Pot.
2. Add water, heavy cream, sugar, and farro.
3. Mix the ingredients with the help of the spoon and close the lid.
4. Cook the farro on low for 6 hours.

Nutrition Info:

- Per Serving: 208 calories, 5.1g protein, 31g carbohydrates, 7.4g fat, 2.2g fiber, 27mg cholesterol, 32mg sodium, 24mg potassium.

Cauliflower Mashed Sweet Potato

Servings: 6
Cooking Time: 6 1/4 Hours

Ingredients:

- 1 head cauliflower, cut into florets
- 1 pound sweet potatoes, peeled and cubed
- 1 shallot, chopped
- 2 garlic cloves, chopped
- 1 cup vegetable stock
- Salt and pepper to taste

Directions:

1. Combine all the ingredients in your Crock Pot.
2. Add salt and pepper to taste and cook on low settings for 6 hours.
3. When done, mash the mix with a potato masher and serve warm.

Cod And Asparagus

Servings: 4
Cooking Time: 2 Hours

Ingredients:

- 4 cod fillets, boneless
- 1 bunch asparagus
- 12 tablespoons lemon juice
- Salt and black pepper to the taste
- 2 tablespoons olive oil

Directions:

1. Divide cod fillets between tin foil pieces, top each with asparagus spears, lemon juice, lemon pepper and oil and wrap them.

2. Arrange wrapped fish in your Crock Pot, cover and cook on High for 2 hours.

3. Unwrap fish, divide it and asparagus between plates and serve for lunch.

Nutrition Info:

- calories 202, fat 3, fiber 6, carbs 7, protein 3

Three Pepper Roasted Pork Tenderloin

Servings: 8

Cooking Time: 8 1/4 Hours

Ingredients:

- 3 pounds pork tenderloin
- 2 tablespoons Dijon mustard
- 1/4 cup three pepper mix
- Salt and pepper to taste
- 1 cup chicken stock

Directions:

1. Season the pork with salt and pepper.

2. Brush the meat with mustard. Spread the pepper mix on your chopping board then roll the pork through this mixture, making sure to coat it well.

3. Place carefully in your crock pot and pour in the stock.

4. Cook on low settings for 8 hours.

5. Serve the pork tenderloin sliced and warm with your favorite side dish.

Mango Chutney Pork Chops

Servings: 4

Cooking Time: 5 1/4 Hours

Ingredients:

- 4 pork chops
- 1 jar mango chutney
- 3/4 cup chicken stock
- 1 bay leaf
- Salt and pepper to taste

Directions:

1. Combine all the ingredients in your crock pot.

2. Add enough salt and pepper and cook on low settings for 5 hours.

3. Serve the pork chops warm.

Salted Caramel Rice Pudding

Servings:2

Cooking Time: 3 Hours

Ingredients:

- 2 teaspoons salted caramel
- ½ cup basmati rice
- 1.5 cup milk
- 1 teaspoon vanilla extract

Directions:

1. Pour milk in the Crock Pot.

2. Add vanilla extract and basmati rice.

3. Cook the rice on high or 3 hours.

4. Then add salted caramel and carefully mix the pudding.

5. Cool it to the room temperature and transfer in the bowls.

Nutrition Info:

- Per Serving: 284 calories, 9.8g protein, 48.9g carbohydrates, 4.7g fat, 0.8g fiber, 16mg cholesterol, 99mg sodium, 161mg potassium.

Crock Pot Steamed Rice

Servings: 8

Cooking Time: 4 Hours

Ingredients:

- 2 cups white rice
- 4 cups water
- 1 bay leaf
- Salt and pepper to taste

Directions:

1. Combine all the ingredients in your crock pot.

2. Add salt and pepper as needed and cook on low settings for 4 hours. If possible, stir once during the cooking process.

3. Serve the rice warm or chilled, as a side dish to your favorite veggie main dish.

Beans And Peas Bowl

Servings:4

Cooking Time: 6 Hours

Ingredients:

- ½ cup black beans, soaked
- 1 cup green peas
- 4 cups of water
- 1 tablespoon tomato paste
- 1 teaspoon sriracha

Directions:

1. Pour water in the Crock Pot.

2. Add black beans and cook them for 5 hours on High.

3. Then add green peas, tomato paste, and sriracha.

4. Stir the ingredients and cook the meal for 1 hour on High.

Nutrition Info:

- Per Serving: 117 calories, 7.4g protein, 21.4g carbohydrates, 0.5g fat, 5.7g fiber, 0mg cholesterol, 23mg sodium, 491mg potassium.

Green Lentils Salad

Servings:2

Cooking Time: 4 Hours

Ingredients:

- ¼ cup green lentils
- 1 cup chicken stock
- ½ teaspoon ground cumin
- 2 cups lettuce, chopped
- ¼ cup Greek Yogurt

Directions:

1. Mix green lentils with chicken stock and transfer in the Crock Pot.
2. Cook the ingredients on High for 4 hours.
3. Then cool the lentils and transfer them in the salad bowl.
4. Add ground cumin, lettuce, and Greek yogurt.
5. Mix the salad carefully.

Nutrition Info:

- Per Serving: 118 calories, 9.4g protein, 17.7g carbohydrates, 1.3g fat, 7.7g fiber, 1mg cholesterol, 395mg sodium, 359mg potassium.

Fragrant Turmeric Beans

Servings:4

Cooking Time: 8 Hours

Ingredients:

- 1 jalapeno pepper, sliced
- 1 oz fresh ginger, grated
- 1 teaspoon ground turmeric
- 2 cups black beans, soaked
- 5 cups chicken stock

Directions:

1. Put black beans in the Crock Pot.
2. Add jalapeno pepper, ginger, ground turmeric, and chicken stock.
3. Cook the meal on low for 8 hours.

Nutrition Info:

- Per Serving: 371 calories, 22.5g protein, 67g carbohydrates, 2.6g fat, 15.9g fiber, 0mg cholesterol, 962mg sodium, 1573mg potassium.

Asparagus Casserole

Servings: 6

Cooking Time: 6 1/2 Hours

Ingredients:

- 1 bunch asparagus, trimmed and chopped
- 1 can condensed cream of mushroom soup
- 2 hard-boiled eggs, peeled and cubed
- 1 cup grated Cheddar
- 2 cups bread croutons
- Salt and pepper to taste

Directions:

1. Combine the asparagus, mushroom soup, hard-boiled eggs, cheese and bread croutons in your Crock Pot.
2. Add salt and pepper to taste and cook on low settings for 6 hours.
3. Serve the casserole warm and fresh.

Tomato Soy Glazed Chicken

Servings: 8

Cooking Time: 8 1/4 Hours

Ingredients:

- 8 chicken thighs
- 1/2 cup soy sauce
- 2 tablespoons brown sugar
- 1 teaspoon chili powder
- 1/2 cup tomato sauce

Directions:

1. Combine all the ingredients in your crock pot.
2. Cook the chicken on low settings for 8 hours.
3. Serve the chicken warm and fresh.

Cheesy Chicken

Servings: 2

Cooking Time: 2 1/4 Hours

Ingredients:

- 2 chicken breasts
- 1 cup cream of chicken soup
- 1 cup grated Cheddar
- 1/4 teaspoon garlic powder
- Salt and pepper to taste

Directions:

1. Combine all the ingredients in your crock pot.
2. Add salt and pepper to taste and cover with a lid.
3. Cook on high settings for 2 hours.
4. Serve the chicken warm, topped with plenty of cheesy sauce.

Apple Cups

Servings:2
Cooking Time: 6 Hours
Ingredients:

- 2 green apples
- 3 oz white rice
- 1 shallot, diced
- ¼ cup of water
- 1 tablespoon cream cheese

Directions:

1. Scoop the flesh from the apples to make the apple cups.
2. Then mix the onion with rice, and curry paste.
3. Pour water in the Crock Pot.
4. Fill the apple cups with rice mixture and top with cream cheese,
5. Then combine the raisins, diced onion, white rice, salt, and curry.
6. Cook the meal on Low for 6 hours.

Nutrition Info:

- Per Serving: 292 calories, 4.1g protein, 65.8g carbohydrates, 2.4g fat, 6g fiber, 6mg cholesterol, 20mg sodium, 310mg potassium.

Oregano Millet

Servings:3
Cooking Time: 3 Hours
Ingredients:

- ¼ cup heavy cream
- ½ cup millet
- 1 teaspoon dried oregano
- 1 cup of water

Directions:

1. Put all ingredients from the list above in the Crock Pot.
2. Close the lid and cook on high for 3 hours.

Nutrition Info:

- Per Serving: 162 calories, 3.9g protein, 24.9g carbohydrates, 5.2g fat, 3g fiber, 14mg cholesterol, 6mg sodium, 81mg potassium.

Milky Semolina

Servings:2
Cooking Time: 1 Hour
Ingredients:

- ¼ cup semolina
- 1 ½ cup milk
- 1 teaspoon vanilla extract
- 1 teaspoon sugar

Directions:

1. Put all ingredients in the Crock Pot.
2. Close the lid and cook the semolina on high for 1 hour.
3. When the meal is cooked, carefully stir it and cool it to room temperature.

Nutrition Info:

- Per Serving: 180 calories, 8.7g protein, 26.5g carbohydrates, 4g fat, 0.8g fiber, 15mg cholesterol, 87mg sodium, 147mg potassium.

Creamed Sweet Corn

Servings: 6
Cooking Time: 3 1/4 Hours
Ingredients:

- 2 cans (15 oz.) sweet corn, drained
- 1 cup cream cheese
- 1 cup grated Cheddar cheese
- 1/2 cup heavy cream
- Salt and pepper to taste
- 1 pinch nutmeg

Directions:

1. Combine the corn, cream cheese, Cheddar and cream in your Crock Pot.
2. Add the nutmeg, salt and pepper and cook on low settings for 3 hours.
3. Serve the creamed corn warm.

Parmesan Artichokes

Servings: 2
Cooking Time: 4 1/4 Hours
Ingredients:

- 2 large artichokes
- 1/4 cup breadcrumbs
- 1/2 cup grated Parmesan
- 1/2 cup vegetable stock

Directions:

1. Cut and clean the artichokes.
2. Mix the breadcrumbs and cheese in a bowl.
3. Top each artichoke with this mixture and rub it well to make sure it sticks to the artichoke.
4. Place the artichokes in a crock pot and add the stock.
5. Cook on low settings for 4 hours.
6. Serve the artichokes warm.

Ginger Glazed Tofu

Servings: 6
Cooking Time: 2 1/4 Hours
Ingredients:

- 12 oz. firm tofu, cubed
- 1 tablespoon hot sauce
- 1 teaspoon grated ginger
- 2 tablespoons soy sauce
- 1/2 cup vegetable stock

Directions:

1. Season the tofu with hot sauce, ginger and soy sauce. Place the tofu in your crock pot.
2. Add the stock and cook on high settings for 2 hours.
3. Serve the tofu warm with your favorite side dish.

Cumin Rice

Servings:6
Cooking Time: 3.5 Hours
Ingredients:

- 2 cups long-grain rice
- 5 cups chicken stock
- 1 teaspoon cumin seeds
- 1 teaspoon olive oil
- 1 tablespoon cream cheese

Directions:

1. Heat the olive oil in the skillet.
2. Add cumin seeds and roast them for 2-3 minutes.
3. Then transfer the roasted cumin seeds in the Crock Pot.
4. Add rice and chickens tock. Gently stir the ingredients.
5. Close the lid and cook the rice on high for 3.5 hours.
6. Then add cream cheese and stir the rice well.

Nutrition Info:

- Per Serving: 247 calories, 5.2g protein, 50.1g carbohydrates, 2.3g fat, 0.8g fiber, 2mg cholesterol, 645mg sodium, 91mg potassium.

Sweet Popcorn

Servings:4
Cooking Time: 20 Minutes
Ingredients:

- 2 cups popped popcorn
- 2 tablespoons butter
- 2 tablespoons brown sugar
- ½ teaspoon ground cinnamon

Directions:

1. Put butter and sugar in the Crock Pot.

2. Add ground cinnamon and cook the mixture on High or 15 minutes.
3. Then open the lid, stir the mixture, and add popped popcorn.
4. Carefully mix the ingredients with the help of the spatula and cook on high for 5 minutes more.

Nutrition Info:

- Per Serving: 84 calories, 0.6g protein, 7.8g carbohydrates, 5.9g fat, 0.7g fiber, 15mg cholesterol, 43mg sodium, 22mg potassium.

Butter Pink Rice

Servings:6
Cooking Time: 5.5 Hours
Ingredients:

- 1 cup pink rice
- 1 cups chicken stock
- 1 teaspoon cream cheese
- 1 tablespoon butter

Directions:

1. Put all ingredients in the Crock Pot and stir gently.
2. Close the lid and cook the meal on low for 5.5 hours.

Nutrition Info:

- Per Serving: 122 calories, 2.2g protein, 22.3g carbohydrates, 3g fat, 1g fiber, 6mg cholesterol, 143mg sodium, 52mg potassium.

Eggplant Parmigiana

Servings: 6
Cooking Time: 8 1/4 Hours
Ingredients:

- 4 medium eggplants, peeled and finely sliced
- 1/4 cup all-purpose flour
- 4 cups marinara sauce
- 1 cup grated Parmesan
- Salt and pepper to taste

Directions:

1. Season the eggplants with salt and pepper and sprinkle with flour.
2. Layer the eggplant slices and marinara sauce in your crock pot.
3. Top with the grated cheese and cook on low settings for 8 hours.
4. Serve the parmigiana warm or chilled.

Coffee Beef Roast

Servings: 6
Cooking Time: 4 1/4 Hours
Ingredients:
- 2 pounds beef sirloin
- 2 tablespoons olive oil
- 4 garlic cloves, minced
- 1 cup strong brewed coffee
- 1/2 cup beef stock
- Salt and pepper to taste

Directions:
1. Combine all the ingredients in your crock pot, adding salt and pepper to taste.
2. Cover with a lid and cook on high settings for 4 hours.
3. Serve the roast warm and fresh with your favorite side dish.

Ginger Slow Roasted Pork

Servings: 8
Cooking Time: 7 1/4 Hours
Ingredients:
- 4 pounds pork shoulder
- 2 teaspoons grated ginger
- 1 tablespoon soy sauce
- 1 tablespoon honey
- 1 1/2 cups vegetables stock
- Salt and pepper to taste

Directions:
1. Season the pork with salt and pepper, as well as ginger, soy sauce and honey.
2. Place the pork in your Crock Pot and add the stock.
3. Cover and cook on low settings for 7 hours.
4. Serve the pork warm with your favorite side dish.

Bacon Millet

Servings:6
Cooking Time: 6 Hours
Ingredients:
- 2 cups millet
- 4 cups of water
- 2 tablespoons butter
- ½ teaspoon salt
- 2 oz bacon, chopped, cooked

Directions:
1. Put millet and salt in the Crock Pot.
2. Add water and cook the meal on low for 6 hours.
3. When the millet is cooked, carefully mix it with butter and transfer in the plates.

4. Add bacon.
Nutrition Info:
- Per Serving: 337 calories, 10.9g protein, 48.7g carbohydrates, 10.6g fat, 5.7g fiber, 21mg cholesterol, 447mg sodium, 186mg potassium.

French Onion Sandwich Filling

Servings: 10
Cooking Time: 9 1/4 Hours
Ingredients:
- 4 pounds beef roast
- 4 sweet onions, sliced
- 4 bacon slices, chopped
- 1 teaspoon garlic powder
- 1/2 cup white wine
- Salt and pepper to taste
- 1 thyme sprig

Directions:
1. Combine all the ingredients in your crock pot.
2. Add salt and pepper to taste and cook on low settings for 9 hours.
3. When done, shred the meat into fine threads and use it as sandwich filling, warm or chilled.

Cherry Rice

Servings:4
Cooking Time: 3 Hours
Ingredients:
- 1 cup basmati rice
- 1 cup cherries, raw
- 3 cups of water
- 2 tablespoons of liquid honey
- 1 tablespoon butter, melted

Directions:
1. Put cherries and rice in the Crock Pot.
2. Add water and cook the meal on high for 3 hours.
3. Meanwhile, mix liquid honey and butter.
4. When the rice is cooked, add liquid honey mixture and carefully stir.

Nutrition Info:
- Per Serving: 249 calories, 3.9g protein, 51.1g carbohydrates, 3.3g fat, 1.4g fiber, 8mg cholesterol, 29mg sodium, 136mg potassium.

Cauliflower Mashed Potatoes

Servings: 4
Cooking Time: 4 1/2 Hours
Ingredients:

* 1 pound potatoes, peeled and cubed
* 2 cups cauliflower florets
* 1/4 cup vegetable stock
* 2 tablespoons coconut oil
* 1/4 cup coconut milk
* Salt and pepper to taste

Directions:

1. Combine the potatoes, cauliflower, stock, coconut oil and coconut milk in your Crock Pot.
2. Add salt and pepper to taste and cook on low settings for 4 hours.
3. When done, mash with a potato masher and serve right away.

Apricot Glazed Gammon

Servings: 6-8
Cooking Time: 6 1/4 Hours
Ingredients:

* 3-4 pounds piece of gammon joint
* 1/2 cup apricot preserve
* 1 teaspoon cumin powder
* 1/4 teaspoon chili powder
* 1 cup vegetable stock
* Salt and pepper to taste

Directions:

1. Mix the apricot preserve with cumin powder and chili powder then spread this mixture over the gammon.
2. Place the meat in your Crock Pot and add the stock.
3. Cook on low settings for 6 hours.
4. Serve the gammon with your favorite side dish, warm or chilled.

Red Salsa Chicken

Servings: 8
Cooking Time: 8 1/4 Hours
Ingredients:

* 8 chicken thighs
* 2 cups red salsa
* 1/2 cup chicken stock
* 1 cup grated Cheddar cheese
* Salt and pepper to taste

Directions:

1. Combine the chicken with the salsa and stock in your Crock Pot.

2. Add the cheese and cook on low settings for 8 hours.
3. Serve the chicken warm with your favorite side dish.

Cider Braised Chicken

Servings: 8
Cooking Time: 8 1/4 Hours
Ingredients:

* 1 whole chicken, cut into smaller pieces
* Salt and pepper to taste
* 1 teaspoon dried thyme
* 1 teaspoon dried oregano
* 1 teaspoon cumin powder
* Salt to taste
* 1 1/2 cups apple cider

Directions:

1. Season the chicken with salt, thyme, oregano and cumin powder and place it in your crock pot.
2. Add the apple cider and cook on low settings for 8 hours.
3. Serve the chicken warm with your favorite side dish.

Butter Buckwheat

Servings:4
Cooking Time: 4 Hours
Ingredients:

* 2 tablespoons butter
* 1 cup buckwheat
* 2 cups chicken stock
* ½ teaspoon salt

Directions:

1. Mix buckwheat with salt and transfer in the Crock Pot.
2. Add chicken stock and close the lid.
3. Cook the buckwheat on High for 4 hours.
4. Then add butter, carefully mixture the buckwheat, and transfer in the bowls.

Nutrition Info:

* Per Serving: 202 calories, 6g protein, 30.8g carbohydrates, 7.5g fat, 4.3g fiber, 15mg cholesterol, 714mg sodium, 205mg potassium.

Bacon Brussels Sprouts

Servings: 6
Cooking Time: 6 1/4 Hours
Ingredients:

- 2 pounds Brussels sprouts, halved
- 6 bacon slices, chopped
- 1/2 cup vegetable stock
- Salt and pepper to taste

Directions:

1. Cook the bacon in a skillet until crisp.
2. Combine all the ingredients in your crock pot, adding salt and pepper to taste.
3. Cook on low settings for 6 hours.
4. Serve the sprouts warm or chilled.

Chicken Drumsticks And Buffalo Sauce

Servings: 2
Cooking Time: 8 Hours
Ingredients:

- 1 pound chicken drumsticks
- 2 tablespoons buffalo wing sauce
- ½ cup chicken stock
- 2 tablespoons honey
- 1 teaspoon lemon juice
- Salt and black pepper to the taste

Directions:

1. In your Crock Pot, mix the chicken with the sauce and the other ingredients, toss, put the lid on and cook on Low for 8 hours.
2. Divide everything between plates and serve.

Nutrition Info:

- calories 361, fat 7, fiber 8, carbs 18, protein 22

French Onion Roasted Pork Chop

Servings: 6
Cooking Time: 6 1/4 Hours
Ingredients:

- 6 pork chops
- 1/4 cup white wine
- 1 can condensed onion soup
- 1 teaspoon garlic powder
- Salt and pepper to taste

Directions:

1. Combine all the ingredients in your Crock Pot.
2. Add salt and pepper to taste and cover with a lid.
3. Cook on low settings for 6 hours.
4. Serve the pork chops warm.

Blue Cheese Chicken

Servings: 4
Cooking Time: 2 1/4 Hours
Ingredients:

- 4 chicken breasts
- 1 teaspoon dried oregano
- Salt and pepper to taste
- 1/2 cup crumbled blue cheese
- 1/2 cup chicken stock

Directions:

1. Season the chicken with salt and pepper and place it in your crock pot.
2. Add the stock then top each piece of chicken with crumbled feta cheese.
3. Cook on high settings for 2 hours.
4. Serve the chicken warm.

Chicken Pilaf

Servings:3
Cooking Time: 6 Hours
Ingredients:

- ½ cup basmati rice
- 2 cups of water
- 5 oz chicken fillet, chopped
- 1 teaspoon chili powder
- ½ teaspoon salt

Directions:

1. Put the rice and chicken fillet in the Crock Pot.
2. Add chili powder, salt, and water. Carefully stir the ingredients and close the lid.
3. Cook the pilaf on Low for 6 hours.

Nutrition Info:

- Per Serving: 205 calories, 16g protein, 25.1g carbohydrates, 3.9g fat, 0.7g fiber, 42mg cholesterol, 443mg sodium, 169mg potassium.

Creamy Polenta

Servings:4
Cooking Time: 2.5 Hours
Ingredients:

- 1 cup polenta
- 3 cups of water
- 1 cup heavy cream
- 1 teaspoon salt

Directions:

1. Put all ingredients in the Crock Pot.
2. Close the lid and cook them on High for 5 hours.
3. When the polenta is cooked, stir it carefully and transfer it in the serving plates.

Nutrition Info:

- Per Serving: 242 calories, 3.5g protein, 31.3g carbohydrates, 11.4g fat, 1g fiber, 41mg cholesterol, 600mg sodium, 24mg potassium.

Beans-rice Mix

Servings:4
Cooking Time: 3 Hours
Ingredients:

- 5 oz red kidney beans, canned
- 1 teaspoon garlic powder
- ¼ teaspoon ground coriander
- ½ cup long-grain rice
- 2 cups chicken stock

Directions:

1. Put long-grain rice in the Crock Pot.
2. Add chicken stock, ground coriander, and garlic powder.
3. Close the lid and cook the rice for 2.5 hours on High.
4. Then add red kidney beans, stir the mixture, and cook for 30 minutes in High.

Nutrition Info:

- Per Serving: 211 calories, 10.1g protein, 41.1g carbohydrates, 0.8g fat, 5.8g fiber, 0mg cholesterol, 387mg sodium, 523mg potassium.

Green Enchilada Pork Roast

Servings: 8
Cooking Time: 8 1/4 Hours
Ingredients:

- 4 pounds pork roast
- 2 cups green enchilada sauce
- 1/2 cup chopped cilantro
- 2 chipotle peppers, chopped
- 1/2 cup vegetable stock
- Salt and pepper to taste

Directions:

1. Combine the enchilada sauce, cilantro, chipotle peppers and stock in your Crock Pot.
2. Add the pork roast and season with salt and pepper.
3. Cook on low settings for 8 hours.
4. Serve the pork warm with your favorite side dish.

Mushroom Rissoto

Servings:4
Cooking Time: 2.5 Hours
Ingredients:

- 1 cup cremini mushrooms, chopped
- 1 tablespoon cream cheese
- 1 cup basmati rice
- 1.5 cups chicken stock

Directions:

1. Put basmati rice and chicken stock in the Crock Pot.
2. Add cremini mushrooms and close the lid.
3. Cook the risotto on High for 2 hours.
4. Then add cream cheese and stir the rice. Cook it on high for 30 minutes more.

Nutrition Info:

- Per Serving: 186 calories, 4.2g protein, 38.1g carbohydrates, 1.4g fat, 0.7g fiber, 3mg cholesterol, 297mg sodium, 142mg potassium

Mustard Short Ribs

Servings: 2
Cooking Time: 8 Hours
Ingredients:

- 2 beef short ribs, bone in and cut into individual ribs
- Salt and black pepper to the taste
- ½ cup BBQ sauce
- 1 tablespoon mustard
- 1 tablespoon green onions, chopped

Directions:

1. In your Crock Pot, mix the ribs with the sauce and the other ingredients, toss, put the lid on and cook on Low for 8 hours.
2. Divide the mix between plates and serve.

Nutrition Info:

- calories 284, fat 7, 4, carbs 18, protein 20

Deviled Chicken

Servings: 4
Cooking Time: 6 1/4 Hours
Ingredients:

- 4 chicken breasts
- 1 cup tomato sauce
- 1/2 cup hot sauce
- 2 tablespoons butter
- 4 garlic cloves, minced
- Salt and pepper to taste

Directions:

1. Combine all the ingredients in your crock pot.
2. Add salt and pepper and cover with a lid.
3. Cook on low settings for 6 hours.
4. Serve the chicken warm and fresh.

Vegetable & Vegetarian Recipes

Paprika Baby Carrot

Servings:2
Cooking Time: 2.5 Hours
Ingredients:
- 1 tablespoon ground paprika
- 2 cups baby carrot
- 1 teaspoon cumin seeds
- 1 cup of water
- 1 teaspoon vegan butter

Directions:
1. Pour water in the Crock Pot.
2. Add baby carrot, cumin seeds, and ground paprika.
3. Close the lid and cook the carrot on High for 2.5 hours.
4. Then drain water, add butter, and shake the vegetables.

Nutrition Info:
- Per Serving: 60 calories, 1.6g protein, 8.6g carbohydrates, 2.7g fat, 4.2g fiber, 5mg cholesterol, 64mg sodium, 220mg potassium.

Hot Tofu

Servings:4
Cooking Time: 4 Hours
Ingredients:
- 1-pound firm tofu, cubed
- 1 tablespoon hot sauce
- ½ cup vegetable stock
- 1 teaspoon miso paste

Directions:
1. Mix vegetables tock with miso paste and pour in the Crock Pot.
2. Add hot sauce and tofu.
3. Close the lid and cook the meal on Low for 4 hours.
4. Then transfer the tofu and liquid in the serving bowls.

Nutrition Info:
- Per Serving: 83 calories, 9.5g protein, 2.5g carbohydrates, 4.8g fat, 1.2g fiber, 0mg cholesterol, 168mg sodium, 176mg potassium.

Garlic Asparagus

Servings:5
Cooking Time: 6 Hours
Ingredients:
- 1-pound asparagus, trimmed
- 1 teaspoon salt
- 1 teaspoon garlic powder
- 1 tablespoon vegan butter
- 1 ½ cup vegetable stock

Directions:
1. Chop the asparagus roughly and sprinkle with salt and garlic powder.
2. Put the vegetables in the Crock Pot.
3. Add vegan butter and vegetable stock. Close the lid.
4. Cook the asparagus on Low for 6 hours.

Nutrition Info:
- Per Serving: 33 calories, 2.3g protein, 6.1g carbohydrates, 1g fat, 2g fiber, 0mg cholesterol, 687mg sodium, 190mg potassium.

Chili Dip

Servings:5
Cooking Time: 5 Hours
Ingredients:
- 5 oz chilies, canned, chopped
- 3 oz Mozzarella, shredded
- 1 tomato, chopped
- ½ cup milk
- 1 teaspoon cornflour

Directions:
1. Mix milk with cornflour and whisk until smooth. Pour the liquid in the Crock Pot.
2. Then add chilies, Mozzarella, and tomato.
3. Close the lid and cook the dip on low for 5 hours.

Nutrition Info:
- Per Serving: 156 calories, 8.7g protein, 22.5g carbohydrates, 5.2g fat, 8.3g fiber, 11mg cholesterol, 140mg sodium, 575mg potassium.

Braised Sesame Spinach

Servings:4
Cooking Time: 35 Minutes
Ingredients:
- 1 tablespoon sesame seeds
- ¼ cup of soy sauce
- 2 tablespoons sesame oil
- 4 cups spinach, chopped
- 1 cup of water

Directions:
1. Pour water in the Crock Pot.
2. Add spinach and cook it on High for 35 minutes.

3. After this, drain water and transfer the spinach in the big bowl.

4. Add soy sauce, sesame oil, and sesame seeds.

5. Carefully mix the spinach and transfer in the serving plates/bowls.

Nutrition Info:

- Per Serving: 88 calories, 2.3g protein, 2.8g carbohydrates, 8.1g fat, 1.1g fiber, 2.8mg cholesterol, 924mg sodium, 213mg potassium.

Brussel Sprouts

Servings:4

Cooking Time: 2.5 Hours

Ingredients:

- 1-pound Brussel sprouts
- 2 oz tofu, chopped, cooked
- 1 teaspoon cayenne pepper
- 2 cups of water
- 1 tablespoon vegan butter

Directions:

1. Pour water in the Crock Pot.

2. Add Brussel sprouts and cayenne pepper.

3. Cook the vegetables on high for 2.5 hours.

4. Then drain water and mix Brussel sprouts with butter and tofu.

5. Shake the vegetables gently.

Nutrition Info:

- Per Serving: 153 calories, 9.2g protein, 10.8g carbohydrates, 9.3g fat, 4.4g fiber, 23mg cholesterol, 380mg sodium, 532mg potassium

Mushroom Steaks

Servings:4

Cooking Time: 2 Hours

Ingredients:

- 4 Portobello mushrooms
- 1 tablespoon avocado oil
- 1 tablespoon lemon juice
- 2 tablespoons coconut cream
- ½ teaspoon ground black pepper

Directions:

1. Slice Portobello mushrooms into steaks and sprinkle with avocado oil, lemon juice, coconut cream, and ground black pepper.

2. Then arrange the mushroom steaks in the Crock Pot in one layer (you will need to cook all mushroom steaks by 2 times).

3. Cook the meal on High for 1 hour.

Nutrition Info:

- Per Serving: 43 calories, 3.3g protein, 3.9g carbohydrates, 2.3g fat, 1.4g fiber, 0mg cholesterol, 2mg sodium, 339mg potassium.

Cream Of Mushroom Soup

Servings:4

Cooking Time: 3 Hours

Ingredients:

- 1 tablespoons olive oil
- ½ cup onion, diced
- 20 ounces mushrooms, sliced
- 2 cups chicken broth
- 1 cup heavy cream

Directions:

1. In a skillet, heat the oil over medium flame and sauté the onions until translucent or slightly brown on the edges.

2. Transfer into the crockpot and add the mushrooms and chicken broth. Season with salt and pepper to taste.

3. Close the lid and cook on low for 6 hours or on high for 3 hours until the mushrooms are soft

4. Halfway before the cooking time ends, stir in the heavy cream.

Nutrition Info:

- Calories per serving: 229; Carbohydrates: 9g; Protein: 5g; Fat: 21g; Sugar:3 g; Sodium:214 mg; Fiber: 2g

Apples Sauté

Servings:4

Cooking Time: 2 Hours

Ingredients:

- 4 cups apples, chopped
- 1 cup of water
- 1 teaspoon ground cinnamon
- 1 teaspoon sugar

Directions:

1. Put all ingredients in the Crock Pot.

2. Cook the apple sauté for 2 hours on High.

3. When the meal is cooked, let it cool until warm.

Nutrition Info:

- Per Serving: 121 calories, 0.6g protein, 32.3g carbohydrates, 0.4g fat, 5.7g fiber, 0mg cholesterol, 4mg sodium, 242mg potassium.

Ranch Broccoli

Servings: 3
Cooking Time: 1.5 Hours
Ingredients:

- 3 cups broccoli
- 1 teaspoon chili flakes
- 2 tablespoons ranch dressing
- 2 cups of water

Directions:

1. Put the broccoli in the Crock Pot.
2. Add water and close the lid.
3. Cook the broccoli on high for 1.5 hours.
4. Then drain water and transfer the broccoli in the bowl.
5. Sprinkle it with chili flakes and ranch dressing. Shake the meal gently.

Nutrition Info:

- Per Serving: 34 calories, 2.7g protein, 6.6g carbohydrates, 0.3g fat, 2.4g fiber, 0mg cholesterol, 91mg sodium, 291mg potassium.

Tomato Okra

Servings: 2
Cooking Time: 6 Hours
Ingredients:

- 2 cups okra, sliced
- 1 teaspoon chili powder
- 1 teaspoon salt
- 1 cup tomato juice
- ¼ cup fresh parsley, chopped

Directions:

1. Put all ingredients in the Crock Pot and carefully mix.
2. Close the lid and cook the okra on Low for 6 hours.

Nutrition Info:

- Per Serving: 67 calories, 3.2g protein, 13.8g carbohydrates, 0.5g fat, 4.4g fiber, 0mg cholesterol, 1514mg sodium, 644mg potassium.

Sesame Asparagus

Servings: 4
Cooking Time: 3 Hours
Ingredients:

- 1-pound asparagus
- ½ cup of soy sauce
- ½ cup vegetable stock
- 1 teaspoon sesame seeds
- 1 tablespoon vegan butter

Directions:

1. Trim the asparagus and put it in the Crock Pot.
2. Add soy sauce and vegetable stock.
3. Then add sesame seeds and butter.
4. Close the lid and cook the meal on High for 3 hours.

Nutrition Info:

- Per Serving: 71 calories, 4.7g protein, 7.1g carbohydrates, 3.5g fat, 2.7g fiber, 8mg cholesterol, 1915mg sodium, 304mg potassium.

Crockpot Baked Tofu

Servings: 4
Cooking Time: 2 Hours
Ingredients:

- 1 small package extra firm tofu, sliced
- 3 tablespoons soy sauce
- 1 tablespoon sesame oil
- 2 teaspoons minced garlic
- Juice from ½ lemon, freshly squeezed

Directions:

1. In a deep dish, mix together the soy sauce, sesame oil, garlic, and lemon. Add a few tablespoons of water if the sauce is too thick.
2. Marinate the tofu slices for at least 2 hours.
3. Line the crockpot with foil and grease it with cooking spray.
4. Place the slices of marinated tofu into the crockpot.
5. Cook on low for 4 hours or on high for 2 hours.
6. Make sure that the tofu slices have a crispy outer texture.

Nutrition Info:

- Calories per serving: 145; Carbohydrates: 4.1g; Protein: 11.6g; Fat: 10.8g; Sugar: 0.6g; Sodium: 142mg; Fiber: 1.5 g

Green Peas Puree

Servings: 2
Cooking Time: 1 Hour
Ingredients:

- 2 cups green peas, frozen
- 1 tablespoon coconut oil
- 1 teaspoon smoked paprika
- 1 cup vegetable stock

Directions:

1. Put green peas, smoked paprika, and vegetable stock in the Crock Pot.
2. Cook the ingredients in high for 1 hour.
3. Then drain the liquid and mash the green peas with the help of the potato masher.
4. Add coconut oil and carefully stir the cooked puree.

Nutrition Info:

- Per Serving: 184 calories, 8.4g protein, 21.9g carbohydrates, 7.8g fat, 7.8g fiber, 0mg cholesterol, 389mg sodium, 386mg potassium.

Sautéed Greens

Servings:4
Cooking Time: 1 Hour

Ingredients:

- 1 cup spinach, chopped
- 2 cups collard greens, chopped
- 1 cup Swiss chard, chopped
- 2 cups of water
- ½ cup half and half

Directions:

1. Put spinach, collard greens, and Swiss chard in the Crock Pot.
2. Add water and close the lid.
3. Cook the greens on High for 1 hour.
4. Then drain water and transfer the greens in the bowl.
5. Bring the half and half to boil and pour over greens.
6. Carefully mix the greens.

Nutrition Info:

- Per Serving: 49 calories, 1.8g protein, 3.2g carbohydrates, 3.7g fat, 1.1g fiber, 11mg cholesterol, 45mg sodium, 117mg potassium.

Coconut Cauliflower Florets

Servings:4
Cooking Time: 4 Hours

Ingredients:

- 2 cups cauliflower, florets
- 1 cup of coconut milk
- 1 tablespoon coconut flakes
- 1 teaspoon salt
- 1 teaspoon ground turmeric

Directions:

1. Sprinkle the cauliflower florets with ground turmeric and salt, and transfer in the Crock Pot.
2. Add coconut flakes and coconut milk.
3. Close the lid and cook the meal on Low for 4 hours.
4. Carefully mix the cauliflower before serving.

Nutrition Info:

- Per Serving: 157 calories, 24.g protein, 6.5g carbohydrates, 14.8g fat, 2.8g fiber, 0mg cholesterol, 606mg sodium, 328mg potassium.

Garlic Sweet Potato

Servings:4
Cooking Time: 6 Hours

Ingredients:

- 2-pounds sweet potatoes, chopped
- 1 teaspoon minced garlic
- 2 tablespoons vegan butter
- 1 teaspoon salt
- 3 cups of water

Directions:

1. Pour water in the Crock Pot. Add sweet potatoes.
2. Then add salt and close the lid.
3. Cook the sweet potato on Low for 6 hours.
4. After this, drain the water and transfer the vegetables in the big bowl.
5. Add minced garlic and butter. Carefully stir the sweet potatoes until butter is melted.

Nutrition Info:

- Per Serving: 320 calories, 3.6g protein, 63.5g carbohydrates, 6.2g fat, 9.3g fiber, 15mg cholesterol, 648mg sodium, 1857mg potassium.

Baked Onions

Servings:4
Cooking Time: 2 Hours

Ingredients:

- 4 onions, peeled
- 1 tablespoon coconut oil
- 1 teaspoon salt
- 1 teaspoon brown sugar
- 1 cup coconut cream

Directions:

1. Put coconut oil in the Crock Pot.
2. Then make the small cuts in the onions with the help of the knife and put in the Crock Pot in one layer.
3. Sprinkle the vegetables with salt, and brown sugar.
4. Add coconut cream and close the lid.
5. Cook the onions on High for 2 hours.

Nutrition Info:

- Per Serving: 214 calories, 2.6g protein, 14.3g carbohydrates, 17.8g fat, 3.7g fiber, 0mg cholesterol, 595mg sodium, 320mg potassium.

Butter Asparagus

Servings:4
Cooking Time: 5 Hours
Ingredients:
- 1-pound asparagus
- 2 tablespoons vegan butter
- 1 teaspoon ground black pepper
- 1 cup vegetable stock

Directions:
1. Pour the vegetable stock in the Crock Pot.
2. Chop the asparagus roughly and add in the Crock Pot.
3. Close the lid and cook the asparagus for 5 hours on Low.
4. Then drain water and transfer the asparagus in the bowl.
5. Sprinkle it with ground black pepper and butter.

Nutrition Info:
- Per Serving: 77 calories, 2.8g protein, 4.9g carbohydrates, 6.1g fat, 2.5g fiber, 15mg cholesterol, 234mg sodium, 241mg potassium.

Cauliflower Curry

Servings:4
Cooking Time: 2 Hours
Ingredients:
- 4 cups cauliflower
- 1 tablespoon curry paste
- 2 cups of coconut milk

Directions:
1. In the mixing bowl mix coconut milk with curry paste until smooth.
2. Put cauliflower in the Crock Pot.
3. Pour the curry liquid over the cauliflower and close the lid.
4. Cook the meal on High for 2 hours.

Nutrition Info:
- Per Serving: 236 calories, 4.9g protein, 13g carbohydrates, 30.9g fat, 5.1g fiber, 0mg cholesterol, 48mg sodium, 619mg potassium.

Corn Pudding

Servings:4
Cooking Time: 5 Hours
Ingredients:
- 3 cups corn kernels
- 2 cups heavy cream
- 3 tablespoons muffin mix
- 1 oz Parmesan, grated

Directions:
1. Mix heavy cream with muffin mix and pour the liquid in the Crock Pot.
2. Add corn kernels and Parmesan. Stir the mixture well.
3. Close the lid and cook the pudding on Low for 5 hours.

Nutrition Info:
- Per Serving: 371 calories, 21.8g protein, 31.4g carbohydrates, 26.3g fat, 3.2g fiber, 87mg cholesterol, 180mg sodium, 378mg potassium.

Broccoli And Cheese Casserole

Servings:4
Cooking Time: 4 Hours
Ingredients:
- ¾ cup almond flour
- 1 head of broccoli, cut into florets
- 2 large eggs, beaten
- Salt and pepper to taste
- ½ cup mozzarella cheese

Directions:
1. Place the almond flour and broccoli in the crockpot.
2. Stir in the eggs and season with salt and pepper to taste.
3. Sprinkle with mozzarella cheese.
4. Close the lid and cook on low for 4 hours or on high for 2 hours.

Nutrition Info:
- Calories per serving: 78; Carbohydrates: 4g; Protein: 8.2g; Fat:5.8 g; Sugar: 0g; Sodium: 231mg; Fiber:2.3 g

Paprika Okra

Servings:4
Cooking Time: 40 Minutes
Ingredients:
- 4 cups okra, sliced
- 1 tablespoon smoked paprika
- 1 teaspoon salt
- 2 tablespoons coconut oil
- 1 cup organic almond milk

Directions:
1. Pour almond milk in the Crock Pot.
2. Add coconut oil, salt, and smoked paprika.
3. Then add sliced okra and gently mix the ingredients.
4. Cook the okra on High for 40 minutes. Then cooked okra should be tender but not soft.

Nutrition Info:

- Per Serving: 119 calories, 2.4g protein, 10.4g carbohydrates, 7.8g fat, 3.9g fiber, 0mg cholesterol, 624mg sodium, 340mg potassium.

Artichoke Dip

Servings:6
Cooking Time: 6 Hours
Ingredients:

- 2 cups Cheddar cheese, shredded
- 1 cup of coconut milk
- 1-pound artichoke, drained, chopped
- 1 tablespoon Ranch dressing

Directions:

1. Put all ingredients in the Crock Pot.
2. Mix them gently and close the lid.
3. Cook the artichoke dip on Low for 6 hours.

Nutrition Info:

- Per Serving: 280 calories, 12.8g protein, 10.8g carbohydrates, 22.1g fat, 5g fiber, 40mg cholesterol, 325mg sodium, 422mg potassium.

Egg Cauliflower

Servings:2
Cooking Time: 4 Hours
Ingredients:

- 2 cups cauliflower, shredded
- 4 eggs, beaten
- 1 tablespoon vegan butter
- ½ teaspoon salt

Directions:

1. Mix eggs with salt.
2. Put the shredded cauliflower in the Crock Pot.
3. Add eggs and vegan butter. Gently mix the mixture.
4. Close the lid and cook the meal on low for 4 hours. Stir the cauliflower with the help of the fork every 1 hour.

Nutrition Info:

- Per Serving: 176 calories, 13.5g protein, 9.9g carbohydrates, 9.7g fat, 2.6g fiber, 372mg cholesterol, 746mg sodium, 421mg potassium.

Garlic Gnocchi

Servings:4
Cooking Time: 3 Hours
Ingredients:

- 2 cups mozzarella, shredded
- 3 egg yolks, beaten
- 1 teaspoon garlic, minced

- ½ cup heavy cream
- Salt and pepper to taste

Directions:

1. In a mixing bowl, combine the mozzarella and egg yolks.
2. Form gnocchi balls and place in the fridge to set.
3. Boil a pot of water over high flame and drop the gnocchi balls for 30 seconds. Take them out and transfer to the crockpot.
4. Into the crockpot add the garlic and heavy cream.
5. Season with salt and pepper to taste.
6. Close the lid and cook on low for 3 hours or on high for 1 hour.

Nutrition Info:

- Calories per serving: 178; Carbohydrates: 4.1g; Protein:20.5 g; Fat: 8.9g; Sugar:0.3g; Sodium: 421mg; Fiber: 2.1g

Spinach With Halloumi Cheese Casserole

Servings:4
Cooking Time: 2 Hours
Ingredients:

- 1 package spinach, rinsed
- ½ cup walnuts, chopped
- Salt and pepper to taste
- 1 tablespoon balsamic vinegar
- 1 ½ cups halloumi cheese, grated

Directions:

1. Place spinach and walnuts in the crockpot.
2. Season with salt and pepper. Drizzle with balsamic vinegar.
3. Top with halloumi cheese and cook on low for 2 hours or on high for 30 minutes

Nutrition Info:

- Calories per serving: 560; Carbohydrates: 7g; Protein:21 g; Fat: 47g; Sugar:2.1 g; Sodium: 231mg; Fiber:3 g

Spicy Eggplant With Red Pepper And Parsley

Servings:4

Cooking Time: 3 Hours

Ingredients:

- 1 large eggplant, sliced
- 2 tablespoons parsley, chopped
- 1 big red bell pepper, chopped
- Salt and pepper to taste
- 2 tablespoons balsamic vinegar

Directions:

1. Place all ingredients in a mixing bowl.
2. Toss to coat ingredients.
3. Place in the crockpot and cook on low for 3 hours or on high for 1 hour.

Nutrition Info:

- Calories per serving: 52; Carbohydrates:11.67 g; Protein:1.8 g; Fat:0.31 g; Sugar: 0.2g; Sodium: 142mg; Fiber: 9.4g

Vegetarian Red Coconut Curry

Servings:4

Cooking Time: 3 Hours

Ingredients:

- 1 cup broccoli florets
- 1 large handful spinach, rinsed
- 1 tablespoon red curry paste
- 1 cup coconut cream
- 1 teaspoon garlic, minced

Directions:

1. Combine all ingredients in the crockpot.
2. Close the lid and cook on low for 3 hours or on high for 1 hour.

Nutrition Info:

- Calories per serving: 226; Carbohydrates: 8g; Protein: 5.2g; Fat:21.4 g; Sugar: 0.4g; Sodium: 341mg; Fiber:4.3 g

Mashed Turnips

Servings:6

Cooking Time: 7 Hours

Ingredients:

- 3-pounds turnip, chopped
- 3 cups of water
- 1 tablespoon vegan butter
- 1 tablespoon chives, chopped
- 2 oz Parmesan, grated

Directions:

1. Put turnips in the Crock Pot.
2. Add water and cook the vegetables on low for 7 hours.
3. Then drain water and mash the turnips.
4. Add chives, butter, and Parmesan.
5. Carefully stir the mixture until butter and Parmesan are melted.
6. Then add chives. Mix the mashed turnips again.

Nutrition Info:

- Per Serving: 162 calories, 8.6g protein, 15.1g carbohydrates, 8.1g fat, 4.1g fiber, 22mg cholesterol, 475mg sodium, 490mg potassium.

Squash Noodles

Servings:4

Cooking Time: 4 Hours

Ingredients:

- 1-pound butternut squash, seeded, halved
- 1 tablespoon vegan butter
- 1 teaspoon salt
- ½ teaspoon garlic powder
- 3 cups of water

Directions:

1. Pour water in the Crock Pot.
2. Add butternut squash and close the lid.
3. Cook the vegetable on high for 4 hours.
4. Then drain water and shred the squash flesh with the help of the fork and transfer in the bowl.
5. Add garlic powder, salt, and butter. Mix the squash noodles.

Nutrition Info:

- Per Serving: 78 calories, 1.2g protein, 13.5g carbohydrates, 3g fat, 2.3g fiber, 8mg cholesterol, 612mg sodium, 406mg potassium

Thyme Fennel Bulb

Servings:4

Cooking Time: 3 Hours

Ingredients:

- 16 oz fennel bulb
- 1 tablespoon thyme
- 1 cup of water
- 1 teaspoon salt
- 1 teaspoon peppercorns

Directions:

1. Chop the fennel bulb roughly and put it in the Crock Pot.
2. Add thyme, water, salt, and peppercorns.
3. Cook the fennel on High for 3 hours.

4. Then drain water, remove peppercorns, and transfer the fennel in the serving plates.

Nutrition Info:

- Per Serving: 38 calories, 1.5g protein, 9g carbohydrates, 0.3g fat, 3.9g fiber, 0mg cholesterol, 643mg sodium, 482mg potassium.

Zucchini Mash

Servings:2

Cooking Time: 45 Minutes

Ingredients:

- 2 cups zucchini, grated
- 1 tablespoon olive oil
- ¼ cup of water
- ½ teaspoon ground black pepper
- 2 tablespoons sour cream

Directions:

1. Put all ingredients in the Crock Pot and gently stir.
2. Cook the zucchini mash on High for 45 minutes.

Nutrition Info:

- Per Serving: 105 calories, 1.8g protein, 4.6g carbohydrates, 9.7g fat, 1.4g fiber, 5mg cholesterol, 19mg sodium, 320mg potassium.

Buffalo Cremini Mushrooms

Servings:4

Cooking Time: 6 Hours

Ingredients:

- 3 cups cremini mushrooms, trimmed
- 2 oz buffalo sauce
- ½ cup of water
- 2 tablespoons coconut oil

Directions:

1. Pour water in the Crock Pot.
2. Melt the coconut oil in the skillet.
3. Add mushrooms and roast them for 3-4 minutes per side. Transfer the roasted mushrooms in the Crock Pot.
4. Cook them on Low for 4 hours.
5. Then add buffalo sauce and carefully mix.
6. Cook the mushrooms for 2 hours on low.

Nutrition Info:

- Per Serving: 79 calories, 1.4g protein, 3.2g carbohydrates, 6.9g fat, 0.8g fiber, 0mg cholesterol, 458mg sodium, 242mg potassium.

Split Pea Paste

Servings:4

Cooking Time: 2 Hours

Ingredients:

- 2 cups split peas
- 2 cups of water
- 1 tablespoon coconut oil
- 1 teaspoon salt
- 1 teaspoon ground black pepper

Directions:

1. Pour water in the Crock Pot.
2. Add split peas and close the lid.
3. Cook them for 2 hours on high or until they are soft.
4. Then drain water and transfer the split peas in the food processor.
5. Add coconut oil, salt, and ground black pepper.
6. Blend the mixture until smooth.

Nutrition Info:

- Per Serving: 367 calories, 24.2g protein, 59.8g carbohydrates, 4.6g fat, 25.3g fiber, 0mg cholesterol, 600mg sodium, 974mg potassium.

Sugar Yams

Servings:4

Cooking Time: 2 Hours

Ingredients:

- 4 yams, peeled
- 1 cup of water
- 1 tablespoon sugar
- 2 tablespoons vegan butter

Directions:

1. Cut the yams into halves and put them in the Crock Pot.
2. Add water and cook for 2 hours on high.
3. Then melt the butter in the skillet.
4. Add sugar and heat it until sugar is melted.
5. Then drain water from the yams.
6. Put the yams in the sugar butter and roast for 2 minutes per side.

Nutrition Info:

- Per Serving: 63 calories, 0.1g protein, 3.3g carbohydrates, 5.8g fat, 0g fiber, 15mg cholesterol, 43mg sodium, 9mg potassium.

Miso Asparagus

Servings:2

Cooking Time: 2.5 Hours

Ingredients:

- 1 teaspoon miso paste
- 1 cup of water
- 1 tablespoon fish sauce
- 10 oz asparagus, chopped
- 1 teaspoon avocado oil

Directions:

1. Mix miso paste with water and pour in the Crock Pot.
2. Add fish sauce, asparagus, and avocado oil.
3. Close the lid and cook the meal on High for 2.5 hours.

Nutrition Info:

- Per Serving: 40 calories, 3.9g protein, 6.7g carbohydrates, 0.6g fat, 3.2g fiber, 0mg cholesterol, 808mg sodium, 327mg potassium.

Coconut Milk Lentils Bowl

Servings:5

Cooking Time: 9 Hours

Ingredients:

- 2 cups brown lentils
- 3 cups of coconut milk
- 3 cups of water
- 1 teaspoon ground nutmeg
- 1 teaspoon salt

Directions:

1. Mix the brown lentils with salt and ground nutmeg and put in the Crock Pot.
2. Add coconut milk and water.
3. Close the lid and cook the lentils on Low for 9 hours.

Nutrition Info:

- Per Serving: 364 calories, 5.3g protein, 12.1g carbohydrates, 34.7g fat, 4.9g fiber, 0mg cholesterol, 491mg sodium, 382mg potassium.

Masala Eggplants

Servings:2

Cooking Time: 2 Hours

Ingredients:

- ½ cup coconut cream
- ½ cup of water
- 1 teaspoon garam masala
- 2 eggplants, chopped
- 1 teaspoon salt

Directions:

1. Sprinkle the eggplants with salt and leave for 10 minutes.
2. Then drain eggplant juice and transfer the vegetables in the Crock Pot.
3. Add garam masala, water, and coconut cream.
4. Cook the meal on High for 2 hours.

Nutrition Info:

- Per Serving: 275 calories, 6.8g protein, 35.5g carbohydrates, 15.3g fat, 20.7g fiber, 0mg cholesterol, 1186mg sodium, 1414mg potassium.

Vegetarian Keto Burgers

Servings:4

Cooking Time: 4 Hours

Ingredients:

- 2 Portobello mushrooms, chopped
- 2 tablespoons basil, chopped
- 1 clove of garlic, minced
- 1 egg, beaten
- ½ cup boiled cauliflower, mashed

Directions:

1. Line the bottom of the crockpot with foil.
2. In a food processor, combine all ingredients.
3. Make 4 burger patties using your hands and place gently in the crockpot.
4. Close the lid and cook on low for 4 hours or on high for 3 hours.

Nutrition Info:

- Calories per serving: 134; Carbohydrates: 18g; Protein: 10g; Fat: 3.1g; Sugar:0.9g; Sodium:235mg; Fiber: 5g

Garlic Butter

Servings:8

Cooking Time: 20 Minutes

Ingredients:

- 1 cup vegan butter
- 1 tablespoon garlic powder
- ¼ cup fresh dill, chopped

Directions:

1. Put all ingredients in the Crock Pot and cook on High for 20 minutes.
2. Then pour the liquid in the ice cubes molds and refrigerate for 30 minutes or until butter is solid.

Nutrition Info:

- Per Serving: 211 calories, 0.7g protein, 1.6g carbohydrates, 23.1g fat, 0.3g fiber, 61mg cholesterol, 167mg sodium, 68mg potassium.

Sauteed Spinach

Servings:3
Cooking Time: 1 Hour
Ingredients:

- 3 cups spinach
- 1 tablespoon vegan butter, softened
- 2 cups of water
- 2 oz Parmesan, grated
- 1 teaspoon pine nuts, crushed

Directions:

1. Chop the spinach and put it in the Crock Pot.
2. Add water and close the lid.
3. Cook the spinach on High for 1 hour.
4. Then drain water and put the cooked spinach in the bowl.
5. Add pine nuts, Parmesan, and butter.
6. Carefully mix the spinach.

Nutrition Info:

- Per Serving: 108 calories, 7.1g protein, 1.9g carbohydrates, 8.7g fat, 0.7g fiber, 24mg cholesterol, 231mg sodium, 176mg potassium.

Cream Zucchini Pasta

Servings:2
Cooking Time: 2 Hours
Ingredients:

- 2 large zucchinis, trimmed
- 1 cup coconut cream
- 1 teaspoon white pepper
- 2 oz vegan Parmesan, grated

Directions:

1. Make the strips from zucchini with the help of a spiralizer and put in the Crock Pot.
2. Add white pepper and coconut cream.
3. Then top the zucchini with grated vegan Parmesan and close the lid.
4. Cook the meal on low for 2 hours.

Nutrition Info:

- Per Serving: 223 calories, 14.1g protein, 16.3g carbohydrates, 13.4g fat, 3.8g fiber, 43mg cholesterol, 335mg sodium, 904mg potassium.

Sweet Potato Puree

Servings:2
Cooking Time: 4 Hours

Ingredients:

- 2 cups sweet potato, chopped
- 1 cup of water
- ¼ cup half and half
- 1 oz scallions, chopped
- 1 teaspoon salt

Directions:

1. Put sweet potatoes in the Crock Pot.
2. Add water and salt.
3. Cook them on High for 4 hours.
4. The drain water and transfer the sweet potatoes in the food processor.
5. Add half and half and blend until smooth.
6. Transfer the puree in the bowl, and scallions, and mix carefully.

Nutrition Info:

- Per Serving: 225 calories, 5.2g protein, 43.7g carbohydrates, 3.9g fat, 7g fiber, 11mg cholesterol, 1253mg sodium, 1030mg potassium.

Creamy Puree

Servings:4
Cooking Time: 4 Hours
Ingredients:

- 2 cups potatoes, chopped
- 3 cups of water
- 1 tablespoon vegan butter
- ¼ cup cream
- 1 teaspoon salt

Directions:

1. Pour water in the Crock Pot.
2. Add potatoes and salt.
3. Cook the vegetables on high for 4 hours.
4. Then drain water, add butter, and cream.
5. Mash the potatoes until smooth.

Nutrition Info:

- Per Serving: 87 calories, 1.4g protein, 12.3g carbohydrates, 3.8g fat, 1.8g fiber, 10mg cholesterol, 617mg sodium, 314mg potassium

Lazy Minestrone Soup

Servings:4
Cooking Time: 3 Hours
Ingredients:

- 1 cup zucchini, sliced
- 2 cups chicken broth
- 1 package diced vegetables of your choice
- 2 tablespoons basil, chopped
- ½ cup diced celery

Directions:

1. Place all ingredients in the crockpot.
2. Season with salt and pepper to taste.
3. Close the lid and cook on low for 3 hours or on high for 1 hour.

Nutrition Info:

• Calories per serving: 259; Carbohydrates: 13.5g; Protein:30.3 g; Fat: 8.3g; Sugar: 0.4g; Sodium: 643mg; Fiber: 4.2g

Creamy White Mushrooms

Servings:4

Cooking Time: 8 Hours

Ingredients:

• 1-pound white mushrooms, chopped
• 1 cup cream
• 1 teaspoon chili flakes
• 1 teaspoon ground black pepper
• 1 tablespoon dried parsley

Directions:

1. Put all ingredients in the Crock Pot.
2. Cook the mushrooms on low for 8 hours.
3. When the mushrooms are cooked, transfer them in the serving bowls and cool for 10-15 minutes.

Nutrition Info:

• Per Serving: 65 calories, 4.1g protein, 6g carbohydrates, 3.7g fat, 1.3g fiber, 11mg cholesterol, 27mg sodium, 396mg potassium.

Eggplant Parmesan Casserole

Servings:3

Cooking Time: 3 Hours

Ingredients:

• 1 medium eggplant, sliced
• 1 large egg
• Salt and pepper to taste
• 1 cup almond flour
• 1 cup parmesan cheese

Directions:

1. Place the eggplant slices in the crockpot.
2. Pour in the eggs and season with salt and pepper.
3. Stir in the almond flour and sprinkle with parmesan cheese.

4. Stir to combine everything.
5. Close the lid and cook on low for 3 hours or on high for 2 hours.

Nutrition Info:

• Calories per serving: 212; Carbohydrates: 17g; Protein: 15g; Fat:12.1 g; Sugar: 1.2g; Sodium: 231mg; Fiber:8.1 g

Cauliflower Rice

Servings:6

Cooking Time: 2 Hours

Ingredients:

• 4 cups cauliflower, shredded
• 1 cup vegetable stock
• 1 cup of water
• 1 tablespoon cream cheese
• 1 teaspoon dried oregano

Directions:

1. Put all ingredients in the Crock Pot.
2. Close the lid and cook the cauliflower rice on High for 2 hours.

Nutrition Info:

• Per Serving: 25 calories, 0.8g protein, 3.9g carbohydrates, 0.8g fat, 1.8g fiber, 2mg cholesterol, 153mg sodium, 211mg potassium

Curry Couscous

Servings:4

Cooking Time: 20 Minutes

Ingredients:

• 1 cup of water
• 1 cup couscous
• ½ cup coconut cream
• 1 teaspoon salt

Directions:

1. Put all ingredients in the Crock Pot and close the lid.
2. Cook the couscous on High for 20 minutes.

Nutrition Info:

• Per Serving: 182 calories, 5.8g protein, 34.4g carbohydrates, 2g fat, 2.2g fiber, 6mg cholesterol, 597mg sodium, 84mg potassium.

Side Dish Recipes

Mango Rice

Servings: 2
Cooking Time: 2 Hours
Ingredients:
- 1 cup rice
- 2 cups chicken stock
- ½ cup mango, peeled and cubed
- Salt and black pepper to the taste
- 1 teaspoon olive oil

Directions:
1. In your Crock Pot, mix the rice with the stock and the other ingredients, toss, put the lid on and cook on High for 2 hours.
2. Divide between plates and serve as a side dish.

Nutrition Info:
- calories 152, fat 4, fiber 5, carbs 18, protein 4

Rosemary Potatoes

Servings: 12
Cooking Time: 3 Hours
Ingredients:
- 2 tablespoons olive oil
- 3 pounds new potatoes, halved
- 7 garlic cloves, minced
- 1 tablespoon rosemary, chopped
- A pinch of salt and black pepper

Directions:
1. In your Crock Pot, mix oil with potatoes, garlic, rosemary, salt and pepper, toss, cover and cook on High for 3 hours.
2. Divide between plates and serve as a side dish.

Nutrition Info:
- calories 102, fat 2, fiber 2, carbs 18, protein 2

Buttery Mushrooms

Servings: 6
Cooking Time: 4 Hours
Ingredients:
- 1 yellow onion, chopped
- 1 pounds mushrooms, halved
- ½ cup butter, melted
- 1 teaspoon Italian seasoning
- Salt and black pepper to the taste
- 1 teaspoon sweet paprika

Directions:
1. In your Crock Pot, mix mushrooms with onion, butter, Italian seasoning, salt, pepper and paprika, toss, cover and cook on Low for 4 hours.
2. Divide between plates and serve as a side dish.

Nutrition Info:
- calories 120, fat 6, fiber 1, carbs 8, protein 4

Beets And Carrots

Servings: 8
Cooking Time: 7 Hours
Ingredients:
- 2 tablespoons stevia
- ¾ cup pomegranate juice
- 2 teaspoons ginger, grated
- 2 and ½ pounds beets, peeled and cut into wedges
- 12 ounces carrots, cut into medium wedges

Directions:
1. In your Crock Pot, mix beets with carrots, ginger, stevia and pomegranate juice, toss, cover and cook on Low for 7 hours.
2. Divide between plates and serve as a side dish.

Nutrition Info:
- calories 125, fat 0, fiber 4, carbs 28, protein 3

Maple Sweet Potatoes

Servings: 10
Cooking Time: 5 Hours
Ingredients:
- 8 sweet potatoes, halved and sliced
- 1 cup walnuts, chopped
- ½ cup cherries, dried and chopped
- ½ cup maple syrup
- ¼ cup apple juice
- A pinch of salt

Directions:
1. Arrange sweet potatoes in your Crock Pot, add walnuts, dried cherries, maple syrup, apple juice and a pinch of salt, toss a bit, cover and cook on Low for 5 hours.
2. Divide between plates and serve as a side dish.

Nutrition Info:
- calories 271, fat 6, fiber 4, carbs 26, protein 6

Sage Sweet Potatoes

Servings: 2
Cooking Time: 3 Hours
Ingredients:
- ½ pound sweet potatoes, thinly sliced
- 1 tablespoon sage, chopped
- 2 tablespoons orange juice
- A pinch of salt and black pepper
- ½ cup veggie stock
- ½ tablespoon olive oil

Directions:
1. In your Crock Pot, mix the potatoes with the sage and the other ingredients, toss, put the lid on and cook on High for 3 hours.
2. Divide between plates and serve as a side dish.

Nutrition Info:
- calories 189, fat 4, fiber 4, carbs 17, protein 4

Beans And Red Peppers

Servings: 2
Cooking Time: 2 Hrs.
Ingredients:
- 2 cups green beans, halved
- 1 red bell pepper, cut into strips
- Salt and black pepper to the taste
- 1 tbsp olive oil
- 1 and ½ tbsp honey mustard

Directions:
1. Add green beans, honey mustard, red bell pepper, oil, salt, and black to Crock Pot.
2. Put the cooker's lid on and set the cooking time to 2 hours on High settings.
3. Serve warm.

Nutrition Info:
- Per Serving: Calories: 50, Total Fat: 0g, Fiber: 4g, Total Carbs: 8g, Protein: 2g

Pink Rice

Servings: 8
Cooking Time: 5 Hours
Ingredients:
- 1 teaspoon salt
- 2 and ½ cups water
- 2 cups pink rice

Directions:
1. Put the rice in your Crock Pot add water and salt, stir, cover and cook on Low for 5 hours
2. Stir rice a bit, divide it between plates and serve as a side dish.

Nutrition Info:
- calories 120, fat 3, fiber 3, carbs 16, protein 4

Green Beans And Red Peppers

Servings: 2
Cooking Time: 2 Hours
Ingredients:
- 2 cups green beans, halved
- 1 red bell pepper, cut into strips
- Salt and black pepper to the taste
- 1 tablespoon olive oil
- 1 and ½ tablespoon honey mustard

Directions:
1. In your Crock Pot, mix green beans with bell pepper, salt, pepper, oil and honey mustard, toss, cover and cook on High for 2 hours.
2. Divide between plates and serve as a side dish.

Nutrition Info:
- calories 50, fat 0, fiber 4, carbs 8, protein 2

Cumin Quinoa Pilaf

Servings: 2
Cooking Time: 2 Hours
Ingredients:
- 1 cup quinoa
- 2 teaspoons butter, melted
- Salt and black pepper to the taste
- 1 teaspoon turmeric powder
- 2 cups chicken stock
- 1 teaspoon cumin, ground

Directions:
1. Grease your Crock Pot with the butter, add the quinoa and the other ingredients, toss, put the lid on and cook on High for 2 hours
2. Divide between plates and serve as a side dish.

Nutrition Info:
- calories 152, fat 3, fiber 6, carbs 8, protein 4

Chicken With Sweet Potato

Servings: 6
Cooking Time: 3 Hours
Ingredients:
- 16 oz. sweet potato, peeled and diced
- 3 cups chicken stock
- 1 tbsp salt
- 3 tbsp margarine
- 2 tbsp cream cheese

Directions:

1. Add sweet potato, chicken stock, and salt to the Crock Pot.
2. Put the cooker's lid on and set the cooking time to 5 hours on High settings.
3. Drain the slow-cooked potatoes and transfer them to a suitable bowl.
4. Mash the sweet potatoes and stir in cream cheese and margarine.
5. Serve fresh.

Nutrition Info:
- Per Serving: Calories: 472, Total Fat: 31.9g, Fiber: 6.7g, Total Carbs: 43.55g, Protein: 3g

Mexican Avocado Rice

Servings: 8
Cooking Time: 4 Hrs
Ingredients:
- 1 cup long-grain rice
- 1 and ¼ cups veggie stock
- ½ cup cilantro, chopped
- ½ avocado, pitted, peeled and chopped
- Salt and black pepper to the taste
- ¼ cup green hot sauce

Directions:
1. Add rice and stock to the Crock Pot.
2. Put the cooker's lid on and set the cooking time to 4 hours on Low settings.
3. Meanwhile, blend avocado flesh with hot sauce, cilantro, salt, and black pepper.
4. Serve the cooked rice with avocado sauce on top.

Nutrition Info:
- Per Serving: Calories: 100, Total Fat: 3g, Fiber: 6g, Total Carbs: 18g, Protein: 4g

Italian Eggplant

Servings: 2
Cooking Time: 2 Hours
Ingredients:
- 2 small eggplants, roughly cubed
- ½ cup heavy cream
- Salt and black pepper to the taste
- 1 tablespoon olive oil
- A pinch of hot pepper flakes
- 2 tablespoons oregano, chopped

Directions:
1. In your Crock Pot, mix the eggplants with the cream and the other ingredients, toss, put the lid on and cook on High for 2 hours.
2. Divide between plates and serve as a side dish.

Nutrition Info:
- calories 132, fat 4, fiber 6, carbs 12, protein 3

Garlicky Black Beans

Servings: 8
Cooking Time: 7 Hours
Ingredients:
- 1 cup black beans, soaked overnight, drained and rinsed
- 1 cup of water
- Salt and black pepper to the taste
- 1 spring onion, chopped
- 2 garlic cloves, minced
- ½ tsp cumin seeds

Directions:
1. Add beans, salt, black pepper, cumin seeds, garlic, and onion to the Crock Pot.
2. Put the cooker's lid on and set the cooking time to 7 hours on Low settings.
3. Serve warm.

Nutrition Info:
- Per Serving: Calories: 300, Total Fat: 4g, Fiber: 6g, Total Carbs: 20g, Protein: 15g

Lemon Artichokes

Servings: 2
Cooking Time: 3 Hours
Ingredients:
- 1 cup veggie stock
- 2 medium artichokes, trimmed
- 1 tablespoon lemon juice
- 1 tablespoon lemon zest, grated
- Salt to the taste

Directions:
1. In your Crock Pot, mix the artichokes with the stock and the other ingredients, toss, put the lid on and cook on Low for 3 hours.
2. Divide artichokes between plates and serve as a side dish.

Nutrition Info:
- calories 100, fat 2, fiber 5, carbs 10, protein 4

Mexican Rice

Servings: 8
Cooking Time: 4 Hours
Ingredients:
- 1 cup long grain rice
- 1 and ¼ cups veggie stock
- ½ cup cilantro, chopped
- ½ avocado, pitted, peeled and chopped
- Salt and black pepper to the taste
- ¼ cup green hot sauce

Directions:
1. Put the rice in your Crock Pot, add stock, stir, cover, cook on Low for 4 hours, fluff with a fork and transfer to a bowl.
2. In your food processor, mix avocado with hot sauce and cilantro, blend well, pour over rice, toss well, add salt and pepper, divide between plates and serve as a side dish.

Nutrition Info:
- calories 100, fat 3, fiber 6, carbs 18, protein 4

Rosemary Leeks

Servings: 2
Cooking Time: 3 Hours
Ingredients:
- ½ tablespoon olive oil
- ½ leeks, sliced
- ½ cup tomato sauce
- 2 garlic cloves, minced
- Salt and black pepper to the taste
- ¼ tablespoon rosemary, chopped

Directions:
1. In your Crock Pot, mix the leeks with the oil, sauce and the other ingredients, toss, put the lid on, cook on High for 3 hours, divide between plates and serve as a side dish.

Nutrition Info:
- calories 202, fat 2, fiber 6, carbs 18, protein 8

Okra Mix

Servings: 4
Cooking Time: 8 Hours
Ingredients:
- 2 garlic cloves, minced
- 1 yellow onion, chopped
- 14 ounces tomato sauce
- 1 teaspoon sweet paprika
- 2 cups okra, sliced
- Salt and black pepper to the taste

Directions:
1. In your Crock Pot, mix garlic with the onion, tomato sauce, paprika, okra, salt and pepper, cover and cook on Low for 8 hours.
2. Divide between plates and serve as a side dish.

Nutrition Info:
- calories 200, fat 6, fiber 5, carbs 10, protein 4

Roasted Beets

Servings: 5
Cooking Time: 4 Hours
Ingredients:
- 10 small beets
- 5 teaspoons olive oil
- A pinch of salt and black pepper

Directions:
1. Divide each beet on a tin foil piece, drizzle oil, season them with salt and pepper, rub well, wrap beets, place them in your Crock Pot, cover and cook on High for 4 hours.
2. Unwrap beets, cool them down a bit, peel, slice and serve them as a side dish.

Nutrition Info:
- calories 100, fat 2, fiber 2, carbs 4, protein 5

Orange Carrots Mix

Servings: 2
Cooking Time: 6 Hours
Ingredients:
- ½ pound carrots, sliced
- A pinch of salt and black pepper
- ½ tablespoon olive oil
- ½ cup orange juice
- ½ teaspoon orange rind, grated

Directions:
1. In your Crock Pot, mix the carrots with the oil and the other ingredients, toss, put the lid on and cook on Low for 6 hours.
2. Divide between plates and serve as a side dish.

Nutrition Info:
- calories 140, fat 2, fiber 2, carbs 7, protein 6

Dill Cauliflower Mash

Servings: 6
Cooking Time: 5 Hours
Ingredients:
- 1 cauliflower head, florets separated
- 1/3 cup dill, chopped
- 6 garlic cloves
- 2 tablespoons butter, melted
- A pinch of salt and black pepper

Directions:
1. Put cauliflower in your Crock Pot, add dill, garlic and water to cover cauliflower, cover and cook on High for 5 hours.
2. Drain cauliflower and dill, add salt, pepper and butter, mash using a potato masher, whisk well and serve as a side dish.

Nutrition Info:
- calories 187, fat 4, fiber 5, carbs 12, protein 3

Green Beans Mix

Servings: 12
Cooking Time: 2 Hours
Ingredients:
- 16 ounces green beans
- ½ cup brown sugar
- ½ cup butter, melted
- ¾ teaspoon soy sauce
- Salt and black pepper to the taste

Directions:
1. In your Crock Pot, mix green beans with sugar, butter, soy sauce, salt and pepper, stir, cover and cook on Low for 2 hours.
2. Divide between plates and serve as a side dish.

Nutrition Info:

- calories 176, fat 4, fiber 7, carbs 14, protein 4

Garlic Butter Green Beans

Servings: 6
Cooking Time: 2 Hours
Ingredients:
- 22 ounces green beans
- 2 garlic cloves, minced
- ¼ cup butter, soft
- 2 tablespoons parmesan, grated

Directions:
1. In your Crock Pot, mix green beans with garlic, butter and parmesan, toss, cover and cook on High for 2 hours.
2. Divide between plates, sprinkle parmesan all over and serve as a side dish.

Nutrition Info:
- calories 60, fat 4, fiber 1, carbs 3, protein 1

Pink Salt Rice

Servings: 8
Cooking Time: 5 Hours
Ingredients:
- 1 tsp salt
- 2 and ½ cups of water
- 2 cups pink rice

Directions:
1. Add rice, salt, and water to the Crock Pot.
2. Put the cooker's lid on and set the cooking time to 5 hours on Low settings.
3. Serve warm.

Nutrition Info:
- Per Serving: Calories: 120, Total Fat: 3g, Fiber: 3g, Total Carbs: 16g, Protein: 4g

Snack Recipe

Apple Dip

Servings: 8
Cooking Time: 1 Hour And 30 Minutes
Ingredients:
- 5 apples, peeled and chopped
- ½ teaspoon cinnamon powder
- 12 ounces jarred caramel sauce
- A pinch of nutmeg, ground

Directions:

1. In your Crock Pot, mix apples with cinnamon, caramel sauce and nutmeg, stir, cover and cook on High for 1 hour and 30 minutes.
2. Divide into bowls and serve.

Nutrition Info:
- calories 200, fat 3, fiber 6, carbs 10, protein 5

Apple Sausage Snack

Servings: 15
Cooking Time: 2 Hrs
Ingredients:
- 2 lbs. sausages, sliced

- 18 oz. apple jelly
- 9 oz. Dijon mustard

Directions:

1. Add sausage slices, apple jelly, and mustard to the Crock Pot.

2. Put the cooker's lid on and set the cooking time to 2 hours on Low settings.

3. Serve fresh.

Nutrition Info:

- Per Serving: Calories: 200, Total Fat: 3g, Fiber: 1g, Total Carbs: 9g, Protein: 10g

Spinach Dip(2)

Servings: 2

Cooking Time: 1 Hour

Ingredients:

- 2 tablespoons heavy cream
- ½ cup Greek yogurt
- ½ pound baby spinach
- 2 garlic cloves, minced
- Salt and black pepper to the taste

Directions:

1. In your Crock Pot, mix the spinach with the cream and the other ingredients, toss, put the lid on and cook on High for 1 hour.

2. Blend using an immersion blender, divide into bowls and serve as a party dip.

Nutrition Info:

- calories 221, fat 5, fiber 7, carbs 12, protein 5

Spicy Dip

Servings: 10

Cooking Time: 3 Hours

Ingredients:

- 1 pound spicy sausage, chopped
- 8 ounces cream cheese, soft
- 8 ounces sour cream
- 20 ounces canned tomatoes and green chilies, chopped

Directions:

1. In your Crock Pot, mix sausage with cream cheese, sour cream and tomatoes and chilies, stir, cover and cook on Low for 3 hours.

2. Divide into bowls and serve as a snack.

Nutrition Info:

- calories 300, fat 12, fiber 7, carbs 30, protein 34

Corn Dip(2)

Servings: 2

Cooking Time: 2 Hours

Ingredients:

- 1 cup corn
- 1 tablespoon chives, chopped
- ½ cup heavy cream
- 2 ounces cream cheese, cubed
- ¼ teaspoon chili powder

Directions:

1. In your Crock Pot, mix the corn with the chives and the other ingredients, whisk, put the lid on and cook on Low for 2 hours.

2. Divide into bowls and serve as a dip.

Nutrition Info:

- calories 272, fat 5, fiber 10, carbs 12, protein 4

Apple Jelly Sausage Snack

Servings: 15

Cooking Time: 2 Hours

Ingredients:

- 2 pounds sausages, sliced
- 18 ounces apple jelly
- 9 ounces Dijon mustard

Directions:

1. Place sausage slices in your Crock Pot, add apple jelly and mustard, toss to coat well, cover and cook on Low for 2 hours.

2. Divide into bowls and serve as a snack.

Nutrition Info:

- calories 200, fat 3, fiber 1, carbs 9, protein 10

Roasted Parmesan Green Beans

Servings: 8 (4.4 Ounces Per Serving)

Cooking Time: 4 Hours And 5 Minutes

Ingredients:

- 2 lbs. green beans, fresh, trimmed
- 2 tablespoons olive oil
- 1 teaspoon salt and black pepper
- ½ cup Parmesan cheese, grated

Directions:

1. Rinse and pat dry green beans with paper towel. Drizzle with olive oil and sprinkle with salt and pepper. Using your fingers coat the beans evenly with olive oil and spread them out do not overlap them. Place green beans in greased Crock-Pot. Sprinkle with Parmesan cheese. Cover and cook on HIGH for 3-4 hours. Serve.

Nutrition Info:

- Calories: 91.93, Total Fat: 5.41 g, Saturated Fat: 1.6 g, Cholesterol: 5.5 mg, Sodium: 337.43 mg,

Potassium: 247.12 mg, Total Carbohydrates: 6.16 g, Fiber: 3.06 g, Sugar: 3.75 g, Protein: 4.48 g

Lemony Artichokes

Servings: 4 (5.2 Ounces Per Serving)
Cooking Time: 4 Hours And 10 Minutes
Ingredients:
- 4 artichokes
- 2 tablespoons coconut butter, melted
- 3 tablespoons lemon juice
- 1 teaspoon sea salt
- Ground black pepper to taste

Directions:
1. Wash the artichokes. Pull off the outermost leaves until you get to the lighter yellow leaves. Cut off the top third or so of the artichokes. Trim the bottom of the stems. Place in Crock-Pot. Mix together lemon juice, salt, and melted coconut butter and pour over artichokes. Cover and cook on LOW for 6-8 hours or on HIGH for 3-4 hours. Serve.

Nutrition Info:
- Calories: 113.58, Total Fat: 5.98 g, Saturated Fat: 3.7 g, Cholesterol: 15.27 mg, Sodium: 702.59 mg, Potassium: 487.2 mg, Total Carbohydrates: 8.25 g, Fiber: 6.95 g, Sugar: 1.56 g, Protein: 4.29 g

Onion Dip(1)

Servings: 6
Cooking Time: 1 Hour
Ingredients:
- 8 ounces cream cheese, soft
- ¾ cup sour cream
- 1 cup cheddar cheese, shredded
- 10 bacon slices, cooked and chopped
- 2 yellow onions, chopped

Directions:
1. In your Crock Pot, mix cream cheese with sour cream, cheddar cheese, bacon and onion, stir, cover and cook on High for 1 hour.
2. Divide into bowls and serve.

Nutrition Info:
- calories 222, fat 4, fiber 6, carbs 17, protein 4

Salsa Beans Dip

Servings: 2
Cooking Time: 1 Hour
Ingredients:
- ¼ cup salsa
- 1 cup canned red kidney beans, drained and rinsed
- ½ cup mozzarella, shredded
- 1 tablespoon green onions, chopped

Directions:
1. In your Crock Pot, mix the salsa with the beans and the other ingredients, toss, put the lid on cook on High for 1 hour.
2. Divide into bowls and serve as a party dip

Nutrition Info:
- calories 302, fat 5, fiber 10, carbs 16, protein 6

Almond Buns

Servings: 6 (1.9 Ounces Per Serving)
Cooking Time: 20 Minutes
Ingredients:
- 3 cups almond flour
- 5 tablespoons butter
- 1 ½ teaspoons sweetener of your choice (optional)
- 2 eggs
- 1 ½ teaspoons baking powder

Directions:
1. In a mixing bowl, combine the dry ingredients. In another bowl, whisk the eggs. Add melted butter to mixture and mix well. Divide almond mixture equally into 6 parts. Grease the bottom of Crock-Pot and place in 6 almond buns. Cover and cook on HIGH for 2 to 2 ½ hours or LOW for 4 to 4 ½ hours. Serve hot.

Nutrition Info:
- Calories: 219.35, Total Fat: 20.7 g, Saturated Fat: 7.32 g, Cholesterol: 87.44 mg, Sodium: 150.31 mg, Potassium: 145.55 mg, Total Carbohydrates: 4.59 g, Fiber: 1.8 g, Sugar: 1.6 g, Protein: 6.09 g

Bourbon Sausage Bites

Servings: 12
Cooking Time: 3 Hours And 5 Minutes
Ingredients:
- 1/3 cup bourbon
- 1 pound smoked sausage, sliced
- 12 ounces chili sauce
- ¼ cup brown sugar
- 2 tablespoons yellow onion, grated

Directions:
1. Heat up a pan over medium-high heat, add sausage slices, brown them for 2 minutes on each side, drain them on paper towels and transfer to your Crock Pot.
2. Add chili sauce, sugar, onion and bourbon, toss to coat, cover and cook on Low for 3 hours.
3. Divide into bowls and serve as a snack.

Nutrition Info:

- calories 190, fat 11, fiber 1, carbs 12, protein 5

Beer And Cheese Dip

Servings: 10
Cooking Time: 1 Hour
Ingredients:
- 12 ounces cream cheese
- 6 ounces beer
- 4 cups cheddar cheese, shredded
- 1 tablespoon chives, chopped

Directions:
1. In your Crock Pot, mix cream cheese with beer and cheddar, stir, cover and cook on Low for 1 hour.
2. Stir your dip, add chives, divide into bowls and serve.

Nutrition Info:
- calories 212, fat 4, fiber 7, carbs 16, protein 5

Onion Dip(3)

Servings: 2
Cooking Time: 8 Hours
Ingredients:
- 2 cups yellow onions, chopped
- A pinch of salt and black pepper
- 1 tablespoon olive oil
- ½ cup heavy cream
- 2 tablespoons mayonnaise

Directions:
1. In your Crock Pot, mix the onions with the cream and the other ingredients, whisk, put the lid on and cook on Low for 8 hours.
2. Divide into bowls and serve as a party dip.

Nutrition Info:
- calories 240, fat 4, fiber 4, carbs 9, protein 7

Crispy Sweet Potatoes With Paprika

Servings: 4 (3.2 Ounces Per Serving)
Cooking Time: 4 Hours And 45 Minutes
Ingredients:
- 2 medium sweet potatoes
- 2 tablespoons olive oil
- 1 teaspoon Cayenne pepper, optional
- 1 tablespoon nutritional yeast, optional
- Sea salt

Directions:
1. Wash and peel the sweet potatoes. Slice them into wedges. In a bowl, mix the potatoes with the other ingredients. Grease the bottom of Crock-Pot and place the sweet potato wedges in it. Cover and cook on LOW for 4- 4 ½ hours. Serve hot.

Nutrition Info:
- Calories: 120.72, Total Fat: 7.02 g, Saturated Fat: 0.98 g, Cholesterol: 0 mg, Sodium: 37.07 mg, Potassium: 260.14 mg, Total Carbohydrates: 9.06 g, Fiber: 2.57 g, Sugar: 2.9 g

Spinach And Walnuts Dip

Servings: 2
Cooking Time: 2 Hours
Ingredients:
- ½ cup heavy cream
- ½ cup walnuts, chopped
- 1 cup baby spinach
- 1 garlic clove, chopped
- 1 tablespoon mayonnaise
- Salt and black pepper to the taste

Directions:
1. In your Crock Pot, mix the spinach with the walnuts and the other ingredients, toss, put the lid on and cook on High for 2 hours.
2. Blend using an immersion blender, divide into bowls and serve as a party dip.

Nutrition Info:
- calories 260, fat 4, fiber 2, carbs 12, protein 5

Sauerkraut Dip

Servings: 12
Cooking Time: 2 Hours
Ingredients:
- 15 ounces canned sauerkraut, drained
- 8 ounces sour cream
- 4 ounces cream cheese
- 4 ounces corned beef, chopped
- 8 ounces Swiss cheese, shredded

Directions:
1. In your Crock Pot, mix sauerkraut with sour cream, cream cheese, beef and Swiss cheese, stir, cover and cook on Low for 2 hours.
2. Divide into bowls and serve.

Nutrition Info:
- calories 166, fat 14, fiber 1, carbs 4, protein 7

Caramel Dip

Servings: 4
Cooking Time: 2 Hours
Ingredients:
- 1 cup butter
- 12 ounces condensed milk
- 2 cups brown sugar
- 1 cup corn syrup

Directions:
1. In your Crock Pot, mix butter with condensed milk, sugar and corn syrup, cover and cook on High for 2 hours stirring often.
2. Divide into bowls and serve.

Nutrition Info:
- calories 172, fat 2, fiber 6, carbs 12, protein 4

Bean Dip

Servings: 56
Cooking Time: 3 Hours
Ingredients:
- 16 ounces Mexican cheese
- 5 ounces canned green chilies
- 16 ounces canned refried beans
- 2 pounds tortilla chips
- Cooking spray

Directions:
1. Grease your Crock Pot with cooking spray, line it, add Mexican cheese, green chilies and refried beans, stir, cover and cook on Low for 3 hours.
2. Divide into bowls and serve with tortilla chips on the side.

Nutrition Info:
- calories 120, fat 2, fiber 1, carbs 14, protein 3

Slow-cooked Lemon Peel

Servings: 80 Pieces
Cooking Time: 4 Hrs
Ingredients:
- 5 big lemons, peel cut into strips
- 2 and ¼ cups white sugar
- 5 cups of water

Directions:
1. Spread the lemon peel in the Crock Pot and top it with sugar and water.
2. Put the cooker's lid on and set the cooking time to 4 hours on Low settings.
3. Drain the cooked peel and serve.

Nutrition Info:

- Per Serving: Calories: 7, Total Fat: 1g, Fiber: 1g, Total Carbs: 2g, Protein: 1g

Caramel Milk Dip

Servings: 4
Cooking Time: 2 Hours
Ingredients:
- 1 cup butter
- 12 oz. condensed milk
- 2 cups brown sugar
- 1 cup of corn syrup

Directions:
1. Add butter, milk, corn syrup, and sugar to the Crock Pot.
2. Put the cooker's lid on and set the cooking time to 2 hours on High settings.
3. Serve warm.

Nutrition Info:
- Per Serving: Calories: 172, Total Fat: 2g, Fiber: 6g, Total Carbs: 12g, Protein: 4g

Peanut Snack

Servings: 4
Cooking Time: 1 Hour And 30 Minutes
Ingredients:
- 1 cup peanuts
- 1 cup chocolate peanut butter
- 12 ounces dark chocolate chips
- 12 ounces white chocolate chips

Directions:
1. In your Crock Pot, mix peanuts with peanut butter, dark and white chocolate chips, cover and cook on Low for 1 hour and 30 minutes.
2. Divide this mix into small muffin cups, leave aside to cool down and serve as a snack.

Nutrition Info:
- calories 200, fat 4, fiber 6, carbs 10, protein 5

Cheese Onion Dip

Servings: 6
Cooking Time: 1 Hour
Ingredients:
- 8 oz. cream cheese, soft
- ¾ cup sour cream
- 1 cup cheddar cheese, shredded
- 10 bacon slices, cooked and chopped
- 2 yellow onions, chopped

Directions:

1. Add cream cheese, bacon and all other ingredients to the Crock Pot.
2. Put the cooker's lid on and set the cooking time to 1 hour on High settings.
3. Serve.

Nutrition Info:
- Per Serving: Calories: 222, Total Fat: 4g, Fiber: 6g, Total Carbs: 17g, Protein: 4g

Cinnamon Pecans Snack

Servings: 2
Cooking Time: 3 Hours
Ingredients:
- ½ tablespoon cinnamon powder
- ¼ cup water
- ½ tablespoon avocado oil
- ½ teaspoon chili powder
- 2 cups pecans

Directions:
1. In your Crock Pot, mix the pecans with the cinnamon and the other ingredients, toss, put the lid on and cook on Low for 3 hours.
2. Divide the pecans into bowls and serve as a snack.

Nutrition Info:
- calories 172, fat 3, fiber 5, carbs 8, protein 2

Salmon Bites

Servings: 2
Cooking Time: 2 Hours
Ingredients:
- 1 pound salmon fillets, boneless
- ¼ cup chili sauce
- A pinch of salt and black pepper
- ½ teaspoon turmeric powder
- 2 tablespoons grape jelly

Directions:
1. In your Crock Pot, mix the salmon with the chili sauce and the other ingredients, toss gently, put the lid on and cook on High for 2 hours.
2. Serve as an appetizer.

Nutrition Info:
- calories 200, fat 6, fiber 3, carbs 15, protein 12

Almond Spread

Servings: 2
Cooking Time: 8 Hours
Ingredients:
- ¼ cup almonds
- 1 cup heavy cream

- ½ teaspoon nutritional yeast flakes
- A pinch of salt and black pepper

Directions:
1. In your Crock Pot, mix the almonds with the cream and the other ingredients, toss, put the lid on and cook on Low for 8 hours.
2. Transfer to a blender, pulse well, divide into bowls and serve.

Nutrition Info:
- calories 270, fat 4, fiber 4, carbs 8, protein 10

Almond Bowls

Servings: 2
Cooking Time: 4 Hours
Ingredients:
- 1 tablespoon cinnamon powder
- 1 cup sugar
- 2 cups almonds
- ½ cup water
- ½ teaspoons vanilla extract

Directions:
1. In your Crock Pot, mix the almonds with the cinnamon and the other ingredients, toss, put the lid on and cook on Low for 4 hours.
2. Divide into bowls and serve as a snack.

Nutrition Info:
- calories 260, fat 3, fiber 4, carbs 12, protein 8

Beans Spread

Servings: 2
Cooking Time: 6 Hours
Ingredients:
- 1 cup canned black beans, drained
- 2 tablespoons tahini paste
- ½ teaspoon balsamic vinegar
- ¼ cup veggie stock
- ½ tablespoon olive oil

Directions:
1. In your Crock Pot, mix the beans with the tahini paste and the other ingredients, toss, put the lid on and cook on Low for 6 hours.
2. Transfer to your food processor, blend well, divide into bowls and serve.

Nutrition Info:
- calories 221, fat 6, fiber 5, carbs 19, protein 3

White Bean Spread

Servings: 4
Cooking Time: 7 Hours
Ingredients:

- ½ cup white beans, dried
- 2 tablespoons cashews, chopped
- 1 teaspoon apple cider vinegar
- 1 cup veggie stock
- 1 tablespoon water

Directions:

1. In your Crock Pot, mix beans with cashews and stock, stir, cover and cook on Low for 6 hours.
2. Drain, transfer to your food processor, add vinegar and water, pulse well, divide into bowls and serve as a spread.

Nutrition Info:

- calories 221, fat 6, fiber 5, carbs 19, protein 3

Spaghetti Squash

Servings: 6 (6.8 Ounces)
Cooking Time: 6 Hours
Ingredients:

- 1 spaghetti squash (vegetable spaghetti)
- 4 tablespoon olive oil
- 1 ¾ cups water
- Sea salt

Directions:

1. Slice the squash in half lengthwise and scoop out the seeds. Drizzle the halves with olive oil and season with sea salt. Place the squash in Crock-Pot and add the water. Close the lid and cook on LOW for 4-6 hours. Remove the squash and allow it to cool for about 30 minutes. Use a fork to scrape out spaghetti squash.

Nutrition Info:

- Calories: 130.59, Total Fat: 9.11 g, Saturated Fat: 1.27 g, Cholesterol: 0 mg, Sodium: 6.79 mg, Potassium: 399.95 mg, Total Carbohydrates: 13.26 g, Fiber: 2.27 g, Sugar: 2.49 g, Protein: 1.13 g

Dessert Recipes

Orange Bowls

Servings: 2
Cooking Time: 3 Hours
Ingredients:

- ½ pound oranges, peeled and cut into segments
- 1 cup heavy cream
- ½ tablespoon almonds, chopped
- 1 tablespoon chia seeds
- 1 tablespoon sugar

Directions:

1. In your Crock Pot, mix the oranges with the cream and the other ingredients, toss, put the lid on and cook on Low for 3 hours.
2. Divide into bowls and serve.

Nutrition Info:

- calories 170, fat 0, fiber 2, carbs 7, protein 4

Chocolate Mango

Servings: 6
Cooking Time: 4 Hours
Ingredients:

- 1-pound mango, puree
- 2 oz milk chocolate, chopped
- 1 cup coconut cream

Directions:

1. Mix mango with coconut cream.
2. Then transfer the mixture in the ramekins.
3. Top every ramekin with chocolate and cover with foil.
4. Place the ramekins in the Crock Pot and close the lid.
5. Cook the meal on Low for 4 hours.

Nutrition Info:

- Per Serving: 188 calories, 2.3g protein, 19.2g carbohydrates, 12.6g fat, 2.4g fiber, 2mg cholesterol, 14mg sodium, 267mg potassium.

Easy Monkey Rolls

Servings: 8
Cooking Time: 3 Hours
Ingredients:

- 1 tablespoon liquid honey
- 1 tablespoon sugar
- 2 eggs, beaten
- 1-pound cinnamon rolls, dough
- 2 tablespoons butter, melted

Directions:

1. Cut the cinnamon roll dough on 8 servings.
2. Then line the bottom of the Crock Pot with baking paper and put the rolls inside.

3. In the bowl mix sugar, egg, liquid honey, and butter. Whisk the mixture.

4. Pour the egg mixture over the cinnamon roll dough and flatten well.

5. Close the lid and cook the meal on High for 3 hours.

Nutrition Info:

- Per Serving: 266 calories, 4.9g protein, 32.6g carbohydrates, 13.3g fat, 1.4g fiber, 86mg cholesterol, 253mg sodium, 80mg potassium.

Vanilla Pears

Servings: 2

Cooking Time: 2 Hours

Ingredients:

- 2 tablespoons avocado oil
- 1 teaspoon vanilla extract
- 2 pears, cored and halved
- ½ tablespoon lime juice
- 1 tablespoon sugar

Directions:

1. In your Crock Pot combine the pears with the sugar, oil and the other ingredients, toss, put the lid on and cook on High for 2 hours.

2. Divide between plates and serve.

Nutrition Info:

- calories 200, fat 4, fiber 6, carbs 16, protein 3

Stuffed Peaches

Servings:4

Cooking Time: 20 Minutes

Ingredients:

- 4 peaches, halved, pitted
- 4 pecans
- 1 tablespoon maple syrup
- 2 oz goat cheese, crumbled

Directions:

1. Fill every peach half with pecan and sprinkle with maple syrup.

2. Then put the fruits in the Crock Pot in one layer and top with goat cheese.

3. Close the lid and cook the peaches for 20 minutes on High.

Nutrition Info:

- Per Serving: 234 calories, 7.2g protein, 19.7g carbohydrates, 15.5g fat, 3.8g fiber, 15mg cholesterol, 49mg sodium, 360mg potassium.

Cinnamon Plum Jam

Servings:6

Cooking Time: 6 Hours

Ingredients:

- 4 cups plums, pitted, halved
- 1 tablespoon ground cinnamon
- ½ cup brown sugar
- 1 teaspoon vanilla extract

Directions:

1. Put all ingredients in the Crock Pot and gently mix.

2. Close the lid and cook it on Low for 6 hours.

Nutrition Info:

- Per Serving: 71 calories, 0.4g protein, 18.2g carbohydrates, 0.1g fat, 1.2g fiber, 0mg cholesterol, 4mg sodium, 91mg potassium.

Sweet Baked Milk

Servings:5

Cooking Time: 10 Hours

Ingredients:

- 4 cups of milk
- 3 tablespoons sugar
- ½ teaspoon vanilla extract

Directions:

1. Mix milk with sugar and vanilla extract and stir until sugar is dissolved.

2. Then pour the liquid in the Crock Pot and close the lid.

3. Cook the milk on Low for 10 hours.

Nutrition Info:

- Per Serving: 126 calories, 6.4g protein, 16.9g carbohydrates, 4g fat, 3g fiber, 16mg cholesterol, 92mg sodium, 113mg potassium.

White Wine Chocolate

Servings:2

Cooking Time: 3 Hours

Ingredients:

- 1 tablespoon cocoa powder
- 2 teaspoons sugar
- 3 cups white wine
- ¼ cup of chocolate chips
- 1 teaspoon vanilla extract

Directions:

1. Put all ingredients in the Crock Pot.

2. Close the lid.

3. Cook the dessert on Low for 3 hours.

4. Then carefully mix it and pour it in the glasses.

Nutrition Info:

- Per Serving: 289 calories, 1.6g protein, 18.6g carbohydrates, 4.4g fat, 1g fiber, 3mg cholesterol, 23mg sodium, 333mg potassium.

Berry Pudding

Servings:2
Cooking Time: 5 Hours
Ingredients:
- ¼ cup strawberries, chopped
- 2 tablespoons sugar
- 2 cups of milk
- 1 tablespoon corn starch
- 1 teaspoon vanilla extract

Directions:
1. Mix milk with corn starch and pour liquid in the Crock Pot.
2. Add vanilla extract, sugar, and strawberries.
3. Close the lid and cook the pudding on low for 5 hours.
4. Carefully mix the dessert before serving.

Nutrition Info:
- Per Serving: 196 calories, 8.1g protein, 30.2g carbohydrates, 5.1g fat, 0.4g fiber, 20mg cholesterol, 115mg sodium, 171mg potassium.

Matcha Shake

Servings:4
Cooking Time: 40 Minutes
Ingredients:
- 1 teaspoon matcha green tea
- 2 cups of coconut milk
- 2 bananas, mashed
- ¼ cup agave nectar

Directions:
1. Mix agave nectar with coconut milk and matcha green tea. Mix the mixture until smooth and pour it in the Crock Pot.
2. Cook the mixture on high for 40 minutes.
3. Then transfer the mixture in the blender, add mashed bananas and blend the liquid until smooth.
4. Pour the cooked shake in the glasses and cool to room temperature.

Nutrition Info:
- Per Serving: 359 calories, 3.4g protein, 28.3g carbohydrates, 28.8g fat, 4.7g fiber, 0mg cholesterol, 19mg sodium, 527mg potassium.

Cinnamon Apple Butter

Servings: 6
Cooking Time: 6 Hrs.

Ingredients:
- 1 lb. sweet apples, peeled and chopped
- 6 oz white sugar
- 2 oz cinnamon stick
- ¼ tsp salt
- ¼ tsp ground ginger

Directions:
1. Add apples, white sugar, cinnamon stick, salt, and ground ginger to the insert of Crock Pot.
2. Put the cooker's lid on and set the cooking time to 3.5 hours on High settings.
3. Discard the cinnamon stick and blend the remaining apple mixture.
4. Put the cooker's lid on and set the cooking time to 3 hours on Low settings.
5. Serve when chilled.

Nutrition Info:
- Per Serving: Calories: 222, Total Fat: 14.1g, Fiber: 9g, Total Carbs: 27.15g, Protein: 3g

Peanut Sweets

Servings:8
Cooking Time: 4 Hours
Ingredients:
- 1 cup peanuts, roasted, chopped
- 1 cup of chocolate chips
- ¼ cup heavy cream

Directions:
1. Put chocolate chips and heavy cream in the Crock Pot.
2. Cook the mixture on low for 4 hours.
3. Then mix the mixture until smooth and add roasted peanuts.
4. Carefully mix the mixture again.
5. Line the baking tray with baking paper.
6. With the help of the spoon, make the medium size balls (sweets) and put on the baking paper.
7. Cool the sweets until they are solid.

Nutrition Info:
- Per Serving: 229 calories, 6.4g protein, 15.5g carbohydrates, 16.6g fat, 2.3g fiber, 10mg cholesterol, 21mg sodium, 210mg potassium.

Lentil Pudding

Servings:4
Cooking Time: 6 Hours
Ingredients:
- ½ cup green lentils
- 3 cups of milk
- 2 tablespoons of liquid honey
- 1 teaspoon vanilla extract
- 1 teaspoon cornflour

Directions:
1. Put all ingredients in the Crock Pot and carefully mix.
2. Close the lid and cook the pudding on Low for 6 hours.
3. Cool the pudding to the room temperature and transfer in the serving bowls.

Nutrition Info:
- Per Serving: 213 calories, 12.3g protein, 32.7g carbohydrates, 4g fat, 7.4g fiber, 15mg cholesterol, 88mg sodium, 343mg potassium.

Gingerbread

Servings:4
Cooking Time: 5 Hours
Ingredients:
- 4 tablespoons coconut oil
- 1 tablespoon gingerbread spices
- ½ cup flour
- ¼ cup of sugar

Directions:
1. Mix all ingredients in the mixing bowl and knead the dough.
2. Roll it up and cut into the cookies with help of the cookie cutter.
3. Line the Crock Pot with baking paper.
4. Put the cookies in the Crock Pot in one layer and bake them on High for 2.5 hours.
5. Repeat the same steps with remaining cookies.

Nutrition Info:
- Per Serving: 221 calories, 1.6g protein, 24.4g carbohydrates, 13.8g fat, 0.4g fiber, 0mg cholesterol, 0mg sodium, 17mg potassium.

Orange Marmalade

Servings: 8
Cooking Time: 3 Hours
Ingredients:
- Juice of 2 lemons
- 3 pounds sugar
- 1 pound oranges, peeled and cut into segments
- 1-pint water

Directions:
1. In your Crock Pot, mix lemon juice with sugar, oranges and water, cover and cook on High for 3 hours.
2. Stir one more time, divide into cups and serve cold.

Nutrition Info:
- calories 100, fat 4, fiber 4, carbs 12, protein 4

Apricot And Peaches Cream

Servings: 2
Cooking Time: 2 Hours
Ingredients:
- 1 cup apricots, pitted and chopped
- 1 cup peaches, pitted and chopped
- 1 cup heavy cream
- 3 tablespoons brown sugar
- 1 teaspoon vanilla extract

Directions:
1. In a blender, mix the apricots with the peaches and the other ingredients, and pulse well.
2. Put the cream in the Crock Pot, put the lid on, cook on High for 2 hours, divide into bowls and serve.

Nutrition Info:
- calories 200, fat 4, fiber 5, carbs 10, protein 4

Pears Jam

Servings: 12
Cooking Time: 3 Hours
Ingredients:
- 8 pears, cored and cut into quarters
- 2 apples, peeled, cored and cut into quarters
- ½ cup apple juice
- 1 teaspoon cinnamon, ground

Directions:
1. In your Crock Pot, mix pears with apples, cinnamon and apple juice, stir, cover and cook on High for 3 hours.
2. Blend using an immersion blender, divide jam into jars and keep in a cold place until you serve it.

Nutrition Info:
- calories 100, fat 1, fiber 2, carbs 20, protein 3

Granola Apples

Servings:6

Cooking Time: 2.5 Hours

Ingredients:

- 6 apples, cored
- 6 teaspoons granola
- 3 teaspoons maple syrup
- ½ cup of water

Directions:

1. Mix maple syrup with granola.
2. Fill the apples with granola mixture and transfer in the Crock Pot.
3. Add water and close the lid.
4. Cook the apples on High for 2.5 hours.

Nutrition Info:

- Per Serving: 131 calories, 1.4g protein, 35.7g carbohydrates, 1.6g fat, 5.9g fiber, 0mg cholesterol, 4mg sodium, 273mg potassium.

Cinnamon Rice Milk Cocktail

Servings:6

Cooking Time: 1.5 Hours

Ingredients:

- 1 cup long-grain rice
- ½ cup agave syrup
- 3 cups of water
- 1 teaspoon ground cinnamon
- 1 banana, chopped

Directions:

1. Put rice in the food processor.
2. Add water and blend the mixture until smooth.
3. Then sieve the liquid and transfer it in the Crock Pot.
4. Add agave syrup and ground cinnamon. Cook the liquid on High for 1.5 hours.
5. After this, transfer the hot liquid in the food processor.
6. Add banana and blend until smooth.

Nutrition Info:

- Per Serving: 215 calories, 2.4g protein, 51.5g carbohydrates, 0.3g fat, 1.1g fiber, 0mg cholesterol, 24mg sodium, 125mg potassium.

Nutty Caramel Apples

Servings: 6

Cooking Time: 4 Hrs.

Ingredients:

- 6 gala apples, cut in half and deseeded
- 8 oz caramel, package

- 5 tbsp water
- 3 tbsp walnuts, crushed

Directions:

1. Toss the apples with water, caramel, and walnuts in an insert of Crock Pot.
2. Put the cooker's lid on and set the cooking time to 3 hours on Low settings.
3. Serve when chilled.

Nutrition Info:

- Per Serving: Calories: 307, Total Fat: 12g, Fiber: 5g, Total Carbs: 47.17g, Protein: 4g

Braised Pears

Servings:6

Cooking Time: 2.5 Hours

Ingredients:

- 6 pears
- 2 cups wine
- 1 tablespoon sugar
- 1 cinnamon stick

Directions:

1. Cut the pears into halves and put them in the Crock Pot.
2. Add all remaining ingredients and close the lid.
3. Cook the pears on High for 2.5 hours.
4. Serve the pears with hot wine mixture.

Nutrition Info:

- Per Serving: 210 calories, 1.1g protein, 38g carbohydrates, 1.1g fat, 6.5g fiber, 0mg cholesterol, 29mg sodium, 320mg potassium.

Apple Cobbler

Servings:2

Cooking Time: 2 Hours

Ingredients:

- 1 cup apples, diced
- 1 teaspoon ground cinnamon
- ½ cup flour
- 2 tablespoons coconut oil
- ½ cup cream

Directions:

1. Mix flour with sugar and coconut oil and knead the dough.
2. Then mix apples with ground cinnamon and place it in the Crock Pot in one layer.
3. Grate the dough over the apples and add cream.
4. Close the lid and cook the cobbler on High for 2 hours.

Nutrition Info:

- Per Serving: 330 calories, 4.1g protein, 42.1g carbohydrates, 17.5g fat, 4.2g fiber, 11mg cholesterol, 21mg sodium, 180mg potassium.

Chocolate Mango Mix

Servings: 2
Cooking Time: 1 Hour
Ingredients:
- 1 cup crème fraiche
- ¼ cup dark chocolate, cut into chunks
- 1 cup mango, peeled and chopped
- 2 tablespoons sugar
- ½ teaspoon almond extract

Directions:
1. In your Crock Pot, mix the crème fraiche with the chocolate and the other ingredients, toss, put the lid on and cook on Low for 1 hour.
2. Blend using an immersion blender, divide into bowls and serve.

Nutrition Info:
- calories 200, fat 12, fiber 4, carbs 7, protein 3

Choco Liquor Crème

Servings: 4
Cooking Time: 2 Hrs.
Ingredients:
- 3.5 oz. crème Fraiche
- 3.5 oz. dark chocolate, cut into chunks
- 1 tsp liquor
- 1 tsp sugar

Directions:
1. Whisk crème Fraiche with sugar, liquor, and chocolate in the insert of Crock Pot.
2. Put the cooker's lid on and set the cooking time to 2 hours on High settings.
3. Serve chilled.

Nutrition Info:
- Per Serving: Calories: 200, Total Fat: 12g, Fiber: 4g, Total Carbs: 6g, Protein: 3g

Vanilla Crème Cups

Servings: 4
Cooking Time: 3 Hrs.
Ingredients:
- 1 tbsp vanilla extract
- 1 cup of sugar
- ½ cup heavy cream, whipped
- 7 egg yolks, whisked

Directions:

1. Mix egg yolks with sugar, vanilla extract, and cream in a mixer.
2. Pour this creamy mixture into 4 ramekins.
3. Pour 1 cup water into the insert of Crock Pot.
4. Place the ramekins the cooker.
5. Put the cooker's lid on and set the cooking time to 3 hours on Low settings.
6. Serve.

Nutrition Info:
- Per Serving: Calories: 254, Total Fat: 13.5g, Fiber: 0g, Total Carbs: 26.84g, Protein: 5g

Caramel

Servings:10
Cooking Time: 7 Hours
Ingredients:
- 1 cup of sugar
- 1 cup heavy cream
- 2 tablespoons butter

Directions:
1. Put sugar in the Crock Pot.
2. Add heavy cream and butter.
3. Close the lid and cook the caramel on Low for 7 hours.
4. Carefully mix the cooked caramel and transfer it in the glass cans.

Nutrition Info:
- Per Serving: 137 calories, 0.3g protein, 20.3g carbohydrates, 6.7g fat, 0g fiber,23mg cholesterol, 21mg sodium, 10mg potassium.

Apple Dump Cake

Servings: 8
Cooking Time: 4 1/2 Hours
Ingredients:
- 6 Granny Smith apples, peeled, cored and sliced
- 1/4 cup light brown sugar
- 1 teaspoon cinnamon
- 1 box yellow cake mix
- 1/2 cup butter, melted

Directions:
1. Mix the apples, brown sugar and cinnamon in a Crock Pot.
2. Top with the cake mix and drizzle with butter.
3. Cover the pot and cook on low settings for 4 hours.
4. Allow the cake to cool in the pot before serving.

Caramel Apple Tart

Servings:4
Cooking Time: 3.5 Hours
Ingredients:
- 2 tablespoons salted caramel
- 2 apples, sliced
- 1 teaspoon butter
- 5 oz puff pastry
- 1 teaspoon olive oil

Directions:
1. Sprinkle the Crock Pot bowl with olive oil from inside.
2. Then put the puff pastry inside and flatten it in the shape of the pie crust.
3. Grease the pie crust with butter and top with sliced apples.
4. Then sprinkle the apples with salted caramel and close the lid.
5. Cook the apple tart on High for 3.5 hours.

Nutrition Info:
- Per Serving: 291 calories, 3.1g protein, 35.3g carbohydrates, 16.2g fat, 3.2g fiber, 3mg cholesterol, 108mg sodium, 152mg potassium.

Glazed Bacon

Servings:4
Cooking Time: 2 Hours
Ingredients:
- 4 bacon slices
- 1 tablespoon butter
- 3 tablespoons water
- 5 tablespoons maple syrup

Directions:
1. Put all ingredients in the Crock Pot.
2. Close the lid and cook the dessert on High for 2 hours.
3. Then transfer the bacon in the serving plates and top with maple syrup mixture from the Crock Pot.

Nutrition Info:
- Per Serving: 193 calories, 7.1g protein, 17g carbohydrates, 10.9g fat, 0g fiber, 29mg cholesterol, 462mg sodium, 159mg potassium.

Slow Cooked Chocolate Cream

Servings: 6
Cooking Time: 2 1/4 Hours
Ingredients:
- 1 1/2 cups dark chocolate chips
- 1 cup evaporated milk

- 1 cup heavy cream
- 1 teaspoon vanilla extract
- 2 tablespoons butter

Directions:
1. Mix all the ingredients in your Crock Pot.
2. Cover and cook on low settings for 2 hours.
3. Allow the cream to cool before using as a filling or frosting for other desserts.

Amaretto Pear Butter

Servings: 6
Cooking Time: 6 1/2 Hours
Ingredients:
- 4 pounds ripe pears, peeled, cored and sliced
- 1 1/2 cups white sugar
- 1/4 cup dark brown sugar
- 1/4 cup Amaretto liqueur
- 1/2 teaspoon cinnamon powder

Directions:
1. Combine all the ingredients in your Crock Pot.
2. Cover the pot and cook on low settings for 6 hours.
3. When done, pour the batter in your glass jars and seal with a lid while still hot.
4. Allow to cool before serving.

Prune Bake

Servings:4
Cooking Time: 3 Hours
Ingredients:
- 2 cups of cottage cheese
- 5 eggs, beaten
- 1 cup prunes, chopped
- 4 teaspoons butter

Directions:
1. Mix cottage cheese with eggs and blend the mixture until smooth and fluffy.
2. Then put the butter into 4 ramekins.
3. Mix cottage cheese mixture with prunes and transfer in the ramekins with butter.
4. Transfer the ramekins in the Crock Pot and close the lid.
5. Cook the meal on High for 3 hours.

Nutrition Info:
- Per Serving: 316 calories, 23.4g protein, 31.7g carbohydrates, 11.6g fat, 3g fiber, 224mg cholesterol, 564mg sodium, 494mg potassium.

Caramel Sauce Poached Pears

Servings: 6

Cooking Time: 6 1/2 Hours

Ingredients:

- 6 ripe but firm pears, peeled and cored
- 1 1/2 cups caramel sauce
- 1 1/2 cups white wine
- 1 cinnamon stick
- 1 pinch salt

Directions:

1. Combine all the ingredients in your crock pot.
2. Cover the pot and cook on low settings for 6 hours.
3. Allow the pears to cool in the cooking liquid before serving.

Espresso Mousse Drink

Servings:1

Cooking Time: 1 Hour

Ingredients:

- ½ cup milk
- 1 teaspoon instant coffee
- ¼ cup of water

Directions:

1. Mix instant coffee with water.
2. Then pour milk in the Crock Pot and cook it on High for 1 hour.
3. Meanwhile, blend the coffee mixture with the help of the hand blender until you get fluffy foam.
4. Transfer the blended mixture into the glass.
5. Add hot milk.

Nutrition Info:

- Per Serving: 61 calories, 4g protein, 6g carbohydrates, 2.5g fat, 0g fiber, 10mg cholesterol, 59mg sodium, 73mg potassium.

Lemon Cream Dessert

Servings: 4

Cooking Time: 1 Hr.

Ingredients:

- 1 cup heavy cream
- 1 tsp lemon zest, grated
- ¼ cup lemon juice
- 8 oz. mascarpone cheese

Directions:

1. Whisk cream with mascarpone, lemon juice, and lemon zest in the Crock Pot.
2. Put the cooker's lid on and set the cooking time to 1 hour on Low settings.

3. Divide the cream in serving glasses then refrigerate for 4 hours.
4. Serve.

Nutrition Info:

- Per Serving: Calories: 165, Total Fat: 7g, Fiber: 0g, Total Carbs: 7g, Protein: 4g

Lemon Zest Pudding

Servings:2

Cooking Time: 6 Hours

Ingredients:

- 1 teaspoon lemon zest, grated
- 2 cups of milk
- 1 tablespoon corn starch
- ¼ cup of sugar
- 1 teaspoon vanilla extract

Directions:

1. Put all ingredients in the Crock Pot and stir with the help of the hand whisker until corn starch is dissolved.
2. Close the lid and cook the pudding on Low for 6 hours.
3. The pudding is cooked, when it is thick.

Nutrition Info:

- Per Serving: 240 calories, 8g protein, 42g carbohydrates, 5g fat, 0.1g fiber, 20mg cholesterol, 115mg sodium, 146mg potassium.

Sweet Corn Ramekins

Servings:2

Cooking Time: 5 Hours

Ingredients:

- 1 cup sweet corn kernels
- ½ cup coconut cream
- 2 tablespoons condensed milk
- 1 teaspoon butter, softened

Directions:

1. Mix corn kernels with coconut cream and condensed milk.
2. Then grease the ramekins with softened butter.
3. Put the corn kernels mixture in the ramekins.
4. Transfer them in the Crock Pot and close the lid.
5. Cook the meal on Low for 5 hours.

Nutrition Info:

- Per Serving: 283 calories, 5.1g protein, 29.1g carbohydrates, 18.6g fat, 2.9g fiber, 12mg cholesterol, 291mg sodium, 340mg potassium.

Dark Chocolate Cream

Servings: 6
Cooking Time: 1 Hour
Ingredients:
- ½ cup heavy cream
- 4 ounces dark chocolate, unsweetened and chopped

Directions:
1. In your Crock Pot, mix cream with chocolate, stir, cover, cook on High for 1 hour, divide into bowls and serve cold.

Nutrition Info:
- calories 78, fat 1, fiber 1, carbs 2, protein 1

Melon Pudding

Servings:3
Cooking Time: 3 Hours
Ingredients:
- 1 cup melon, chopped
- ¼ cup of coconut milk
- 2 tablespoons cornstarch
- 1 teaspoon vanilla extract

Directions:
1. Blend the melon until smooth and mix with coconut milk, cornstarch, and vanilla extract.
2. Transfer the mixture in the Crock Pot and cook the pudding on low for 3 hours.

Nutrition Info:
- Per Serving: 88 calories, 0.9g protein, 10.4g carbohydrates, 4.9g fat, 1g fiber, 0mg cholesterol, 12mg sodium, 194mg potassium.

Blueberries Jam

Servings: 2
Cooking Time: 4 Hours
Ingredients:
- 2 cups blueberries
- ½ cup water
- ¼ pound sugar
- Zest of 1 lime

Directions:
1. In your Crock Pot, combine the berries with the water and the other ingredients, toss, put the lid on and cook on High for 4 hours.
2. Divide into small jars and serve cold.

Nutrition Info:
- calories 250, fat 3, fiber 2, carbs 6, protein 1

Apple Compote

Servings: 2
Cooking Time: 1 Hour
Ingredients:
- 1 pound apples, cored and cut into wedges
- ½ cup water
- 1 tablespoon sugar
- 1 teaspoon vanilla extract
- ½ teaspoon almond extract

Directions:
1. In your Crock Pot, mix the apples with the water and the other ingredients, toss, put the lid on and cook on High for 1 hour.
2. Divide into bowls and serve cold.

Nutrition Info:
- calories 203, fat 0, fiber 1, carbs 5, protein 4

Caramelized Bananas

Servings:6
Cooking Time: 2 Hours 15 Minutes
Ingredients:
- 6 bananas, peeled
- 2 tablespoons butter
- 3 tablespoons caramel

Directions:
1. Put butter in the Crock Pot.
2. Add bananas and cook them on High for 15 minutes.
3. Then add caramel and cook the dessert on Low for 2 hours.
4. Carefully mix the cooked dessert and transfer it into the plates.

Nutrition Info:
- Per Serving: 159 calories, 1.6g protein, 29.3g carbohydrates, 5.3g fat, 3.1g fiber, 10mg cholesterol, 28mg sodium, 424mg potassium.

Tomato Jam

Servings: 2
Cooking Time: 3 Hours
Ingredients:
- ½ pound tomatoes, chopped
- 1 green apple, grated
- 2 tablespoons red wine vinegar
- 4 tablespoons sugar

Directions:
1. In your Crock Pot, mix the tomatoes with the apple and the other ingredients, whisk, put the lid on and cook on Low for 3 hours.

2. Whisk the jam well, blend a bit using an immersion blender, divide into bowls and serve cold.

Nutrition Info:

- calories 70, fat 1, fiber 1, carbs 18, protein 1

Chocolate Whipped Cream

Servings:4

Cooking Time: 2 Hours

Ingredients:

- ½ cup of chocolate chips
- 1 cup heavy cream
- 1 tablespoon sugar
- 1 teaspoon vanilla extract
- ½ teaspoon lime zest, sliced

Directions:

1. Mix chocolate chips with vanilla extract and put it in the Crock Pot.
2. Close the lid and cook them on Low for 2 hours.
3. Meanwhile, whip the heavy cream and mix it with sugar.
4. Transfer the whipped cream in the serving ramekins.
5. Then sprinkle it with melted chocolate chips.
6. Top every serving with lime zest.

Nutrition Info:

- Per Serving: 230 calories, 2.2g protein, 16.5g carbohydrates, 17.3g fat, 6.4g fiber, 46mg cholesterol, 28mg sodium, 103mg potassium.

Mascarpone With Strawberry Jelly

Servings:6

Cooking Time: 1 Hour

Ingredients:

- 2 cups strawberries, chopped
- 1 tablespoon gelatin
- 3 tablespoons sugar
- ¼ cup of water
- 1 cup mascarpone

Directions:

1. Mix strawberries with sugar and blend the mixture until smooth.
2. Transfer it in the Crock Pot and cook on High for 1 hour.
3. Meanwhile, mix water with gelatin.
4. Whisk the mascarpone well.
5. When the strawberry mixture is cooked, cool it little and add gelatin. Carefully mix it.
6. Pour the strawberry mixture in the ramekins and refrigerate for 2 hours.

7. Then top the jelly with whisked mascarpone.

Nutrition Info:

- Per Serving: 125 calories, 9g protein, 11g carbohydrates, 5.5g fat, 1g fiber, 21mg cholesterol, 45mg sodium, 118mg potassium.

Panna Cotta

Servings:2

Cooking Time: 1.5 Hours

Ingredients:

- 1 tablespoon gelatin
- 1 cup cream
- ¼ cup of sugar
- 2 tablespoons strawberry jam

Directions:

1. Pour cream in the Crock Pot.
2. Add sugar and close the lid.
3. Cook the liquid on High for 1.5 hours.
4. Then cool it to the room temperature, add gelatin, and mix until smooth.
5. Pour the liquid in the glasses and refrigerate until solid.
6. Top every cream jelly with jam.

Nutrition Info:

- Per Serving: 270 calories, 7g protein, 47.4g carbohydrates, 6.7g fat, 0g fiber, 23mg cholesterol, 53mg sodium, 45mg potassium.

Pumpkin Balls

Servings:4

Cooking Time: 2 Hours

Ingredients:

- ½ cup pumpkin puree
- ¼ cup of sugar
- 4 tablespoons flour
- 1 teaspoon olive oil

Directions:

1. Mix pumpkin puree with sugar.
2. Then add flour and knead the soft dough.
3. Make the balls from the pumpkin mixture.
4. After this, brush the Crock Pot bottom with olive oil.
5. Put the pumpkin balls in the Crock Pot in one layer and close the lid.
6. Cook the pumpkin balls on High for 2 hours.

Nutrition Info:

- Per Serving: 96 calories, 1.2g protein, 20.9g carbohydrates, 1.3g fat, 1.1g fiber, 0mg cholesterol, 2mg sodium, 71mg potassium.

Cocoa Peanut Candies

Servings: 11
Cooking Time: 2.5 Hrs.

Ingredients:

- 6 tbsp, peanuts, roasted and crushed
- 8 oz dark chocolate, crushed
- ¼ cup of cocoa powder
- 4 tbsp chocolate chips
- 3 tbsp heavy cream

Directions:

1. Add roasted peanuts and rest of the ingredients to the insert of Crock Pot.
2. Put the cooker's lid on and set the cooking time to 5 hours on Low settings.
3. Divide this chocolate mixture into a silicone candy molds tray.
4. Place this tray in the refrigerator for 2 hours.
5. Serve.

Nutrition Info:

- Per Serving: Calories: 229, Total Fat: 15.8g, Fiber: 3g, Total Carbs: 19.02g, Protein: 5g

Apples With Raisins

Servings:4
Cooking Time: 5 Hours

Ingredients:

- 4 big apples
- 4 teaspoons raisins
- 4 teaspoons sugar
- ½ teaspoon ground cinnamon
- ½ cup of water

Directions:

1. Core the apples and fill them with sugar and raisins.
2. Then arrange the apples in the Crock Pot.
3. Sprinkle them with ground cinnamon.
4. Add water and close the lid.
5. Cook the apples on low for 5 hours.

Nutrition Info:

- Per Serving: 141 calories, 0.7g protein, 37.4g carbohydrates, 0.4g fat, 5.7g fiber, 0mg cholesterol, 3mg sodium, 263mg potassium.

Banana Ice Cream

Servings:2
Cooking Time: 5 Hours

Ingredients:

- ½ cup cream
- 4 tablespoons sugar
- 4 bananas, chopped
- 2 egg yolks

Directions:

1. Mix sugar with egg yolks and blend until you get a lemon color mixture.
2. After this, mix the cream with egg yolks and transfer in the Crock Pot.
3. Cook the mixture on low for 5 hours. Stir the liquid from time to time.
4. After this, mix the cream mixture with bananas and blend until smooth.
5. Place the mixture in the plastic vessel and refrigerate until solid.

Nutrition Info:

- Per Serving: 392 calories, 5.8g protein, 80.4g carbohydrates, 8.6g fat, 6.1g fiber, 221mg cholesterol, 30mg sodium, 885mg potassium.

RECIPES INDEX

Broccoli Omelet 25

Brussel Sprouts 71

Buffalo Chicken Tenders 44

Buffalo Cremini Mushrooms 77

Butter Asparagus 74

Butter Buckwheat 67

Butter Chicken 40

Butter Crab Legs 51

Butter Dipped Crab Legs 56

Butter Pink Rice 65

Butter Salmon 56

Butter Smelt 53

Butter Tilapia 56

Buttered Broccoli 61

Buttery Mushrooms 81

C

Cajun Pork Loin 37

Caramel 96

Caramel Apple Tart 97

Caramel Dip 89

Caramel Milk Dip 89

Caramel Pecan Sticky Buns 26

Caramel Sauce Poached Pears 98

Caramelized Bananas 99

Caribbean Pork Chop 29

Carrot Pudding 17

Cauliflower Curry 74

Cauliflower Mashed Potatoes 67

Cauliflower Mashed Sweet Potato 61

Cauliflower Rice 80

Cayenne Pepper Strips 39

Cheese Onion Dip 89

Cheesy Beef Dip 27

Cheesy Chicken 63

Cheesy Fish Dip 55

Cherry Rice 66

Chia Oatmeal 25

Chicken And Green Onion Sauce 41

Chicken And Sour Cream 49

Chicken Drumsticks And Buffalo Sauce 68

Chicken In Sweet Soy Sauce 42

Chicken Masala 43

Chicken Meatballs 16

Chicken Omelet 22

Chicken Parm 44

Chicken Pate 43

Chicken Piccata 42

Chicken Pilaf 68

Chicken Sausages In Jam 47

Chicken Stuffed With Plums 40

Chicken Vegetable Curry 44

Chicken Wings In Vodka Sauce 46

Chicken With Basil And Tomatoes 45

Chicken With Figs 47

Chicken With Green Onion Sauce 49

Chicken With Peach And Orange Sauce 49

Chicken With Sweet Potato 82

Chicken, Peppers And Onions 50

Chili Bigeye Jack (tuna) 57

Chili Crockpot Brisket 37

Chili Dip 70

Chili Sausages 48

Chili-rubbed Tilapia 52

Chipotle Bbq Sausage Bites 26

Choco Liquor Crème 96

Chocolate Mango 91

Chocolate Mango Mix 96

Chocolate Oatmeal 20

Chocolate Whipped Cream 100

Chorizo Eggs 20

Cider Braised Chicken 67

Cilantro Haddock 59

Cilantro Lime Chicken 49

Cinnamon Apple Butter 93

Cinnamon Catfish 53

Cinnamon Pecans Snack 90

Cinnamon Plum Jam 92

Cinnamon Rice Milk Cocktail 95

Citrus-rubbed Skirt Steak 36

Cocoa Peanut Candies 101

Coconut Cauliflower Florets 73

Coconut Curry Cod 57

Coconut Milk Lentils Bowl 78

Green Beans Mix 85

Green Enchilada Pork Roast 69

Green Lentils Salad 63

Green Peas Puree 72

H

Halved Chicken 46

Ham Pockets 25

Harissa Chicken Breasts 46

Honey Beef Sausages 32

Honey Pumpkin 17

Horseradish Chicken Wings 43

Horseradish Pork Chops 34

Hot Beef 29

Hot Sauce Shrimps 55

Hot Tofu 70

I

Italian Eggplant 83

Italian Style Tenders 41

J

Jalapeno Chicken Wings 50

K

Kale Cups 20

Kebab Cubes 36

L

Lazy Minestrone Soup 79

Leek Bake 20

Leek Eggs 19

Lemon Artichokes 83

Lemon Cream Dessert 98

Lemon Garlic Dump Chicken 47

Lemon Parsley Chicken 42

Lemon Zest Pudding 98

Lemony Artichokes 87

Lemony Chicken 45

Lentil Pudding 94

Light Egg Scramble 18

M

Mackerel Bites 54

Mango Chutney Pork Chops 62

Mango Rice 81

Maple Mustard Salmon 57

Maple Sweet Potatoes 81

Maple Syrup Glazed Carrots 27

Marinara Salmon 53

Masala Eggplants 78

Mascarpone With Strawberry Jelly 100

Mashed Turnips 76

Matcha Shake 93

Melon Pudding 99

Mexican Avocado Rice 83

Mexican Chicken In Crockpot 46

Mexican Rice 84

Milk Pudding 22

Milky Semolina 64

Miso Asparagus 78

Miso-poached Cod 56

Mocha Latte Quinoa Mix 24

Mushroom Rissoto 69

Mushroom Steaks 71

Mustard Cod 53

Mustard Short Ribs 69

N

Naked Beef Enchilada In A Crockpot 30

Nutty Caramel Apples 95

O

Okra Mix 84

Old Fashioned Shredded Beef 36

Olive Eggs 24

Omelet With Greens 18

One Pot Pork Chops 36

Onion Dip(1) 87

Onion Dip(3) 88

Orange Bowls 91

Orange Carrots Mix 84

Orange Marmalade 94

Orange Pudding 16

Oregano Millet 64

P

Sun-dried Tomato Chicken 40

Sweet And Mustard Tilapia 59

Sweet And Sour Shrimps 59

Sweet Baked Milk 92

Sweet Beef 31

Sweet Corn Ramekins 98

Sweet Farro 61

Sweet Lamb Ribs 37

Sweet Milkfish Saute 56

Sweet Popcorn 65

Sweet Pork Shoulder 38

Sweet Potato Puree 79

Sweet Quinoa 22

T

Taco Pork 31

Tender Duck Fillets 41

Tenderloin Steaks With Red Wine And Mushrooms 37

Three Pepper Roasted Pork Tenderloin 62

Thyme And Sesame Halibut 55

Thyme Fennel Bulb 76

Thyme Whole Chicken 48

Tomato Jam 99

Tomato Okra 72

Tomato Soy Glazed Chicken 63

Turkey With Plums 40

Turmeric Mackerel 50

V

Vanilla Crème Cups 96

Vanilla Pears 92

Vegan Milk Clams 51

Vegetarian Keto Burgers 78

Vegetarian Red Coconut Curry 76

Vinegar Chicken Wings 47

W

White Bean Spread 91

White Wine Chocolate 92

Wine Chicken 41

Z

Zucchini Mash 77

Made in the USA
Las Vegas, NV
13 May 2023

71995457R10059